14.15

# THE ANCIENT ROMANS
## HOW THEY LIVED AND WORKED

# The Ancient Romans

## HOW THEY LIVED AND WORKED

O. A. W. Dilke

**DAVID & CHARLES**
NEWTON ABBOT  LONDON  VANCOUVER

Distributed in the U.S. by DUFOUR EDITIONS, INC.

ISBN 0 7153 6553 3

Set in 11 on 13pt Baskerville
and printed in Great Britain
by Redwood Burn Limited, Trowbridge & Esher
for David & Charles (Publishers) Limited
Brunel House   Newton Abbot   Devon

Published in Canada
by Douglas David & Charles Limited
1875 Welch Street   North Vancouver   BC

# Contents

5

# List of Illustrations

**FIGURES**

# Introduction

This book attempts to bring the ancient Romans to life, to recreate their daily existence, and to approach an understanding of the economy of the Roman world from the point of view of the tasks in which the people were occupied. The many remains that survive from the great civilisation of Rome are not just objects to adorn museum cases, but can supply real evidence of the way in which millions of men and women over a vast area lived, worked and played.

Rome started as a small city, but itself grew to about a million inhabitants as the areas in which Romans lived and worked expanded into three continents, where there were very varied types of country and climate. Reconstructing the civilisation of Rome is like working on a multi-layer jigsaw. To piece it together we can use clues gathered from inscriptions and from the many texts which remain out of the even greater number that originally existed.

In the space of this small book only some examples can be quoted of the visible remains, the literary legacy, thought and way of life of this great empire. But even these should suffice to demonstrate its strength, vitality and lasting influence. In comparison, the empires of the Near East were limited in extent, the Greek city-states (brilliant as was much of their achievement) were divided against themselves, the conquests of Alexander the Great were not long-lasting, Carthage was decisively defeated by Rome. Part of the reason for Rome's supremacy was the ease with which its armies could be moved from place to place owing to the excellent roads.

An attempt has been made to interpret concepts which differ from those of the modern world, even though we can draw many parallels with the Roman level of civilisation. Religion, to an early Roman, was related to the need to fulfil obligations rather than to what it implies today. Vocabulary itself can be misleading, since a number of words are common to Latin and English yet have different meanings in each. Thus a magistrate was not concerned merely with legal cases: he was a state official with a whole variety of functions. A consul was not the representative of a foreign power, but one of the two chief magistrates. A colony was not a large dependent overseas territory but a settlement of small-holders, either in Italy or elsewhere. A province refers not, during the classical period, to a governmental division of Italy but to one of the other territories in Europe, Asia or Africa administered by Rome. Republican refers not to a political party but to the period of the Roman Republic, as distinct from the period of the kings before it and the period of the Empire after.

The first part of the book is concerned with the growth, organisation and control of the Roman world. The middle investigates personal lives in the home, work in the fields and towns, and interest in learning and literary activities. The final part attempts to account for the decline and to summarise the legacy of Rome.

I am much indebted to my wife and to Professor Maurice Pope, who is writing the companion volume on the Greeks, for their invaluable help in the composition of this book. I should also like to thank the Roman Society, the British School in Rome and the publishers for assistance received. For photographic material I wish to acknowledge the assistance of the British Museum; the Mansell Collection, London; and the Photography Department of the University of Leeds, whose artist Mr B. Emmison drew several of the diagrams. My wife and son also helped with the compilation of illustrations. Sources of illustrations are indicated on the lists of figures and plates.

# I

# *Rome: How It Started*

In the early period of antiquity the most developed areas of the ancient world, from whose civilisations that of Rome was ultimately derived, were Mesopotamia, the Nile valley and the eastern Mediterranean. Later, Greek colonists and Phoenician traders expanded in Sicily and the coastal regions of the western Mediterranean. As the Italian peoples came into contact with the outposts of these civilisations, they gradually acquired a civilisation of their own, which under the leadership of Rome eventually outstripped the Phoenicians of Carthage, the Greeks and the eastern nations.

## THE SITE

Rome started, as had the Greek city-states, as a very small settlement which developed its own laws and government. The site of Rome (Fig 1), on the left bank of the Tiber, was not at a ford but at a point on the river where the crossing could be controlled. According to Livy, the island in the Tiber, still a prominent feature, originated in an accumulation of mud round harvested grain which had been thrown into the river. It provided a bridging-point, though an earlier one was immediately below it; the bridge to the island, Pons Fabricius, erected in 62 BC, still stands and is used by traffic. Several of the famous seven hills were inhabited before there was any real town. The hills are composed of recent, fairly soft volcanic materials and have been separated by water erosion. They provided dry zones for settlement above the flood-plain of the

Tiber, an area of meander migration, and thus were mainly within the first wall. The nearest alluvial plain became the cattle market, and the large marshy area to the north the training ground for troops.

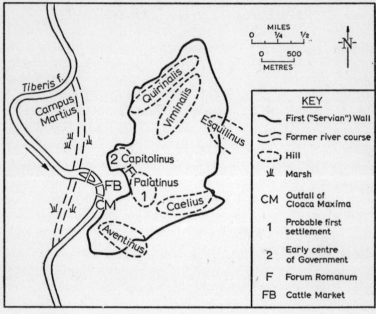

Fig 1    The site of early Rome on its seven hills

Excavation has shown that from the ninth century BC there had been settlements on the Palatine, Esquiline and Quirinal. The keeping of sheep there was one of the earliest occupations, and the flood-plain provided seasonal pasture. But it is also thought that the early inhabitants profited from their position on a salt route up the Tiber.

## LEGEND

The legends about the origins of Rome preserved in classical literature are not necessarily to be trusted. Livy, in the first book of whose history many of them appear, admits that the fabulous element looms large in traditions of the regal period. The famous story of Aeneas' long journey from Troy when it was sacked by the Greeks, his visits to North Africa, Sicily and Cumae, his inspection of the site of Rome and his battles in Latium may have started with the Greek historian Hellanicus (fifth century BC). Roman writers were keen to develop it. This was partly due to a sense of clan pride, which might possibly be compared to the pride of the British monarchy in its descent from Macbeth: Aeneas' son Ascanius, or Iulus, was claimed as ancestor by the Gens Iulia, to which Julius Caesar and by adoption Augustus belonged. Certainly Alba Longa, 30km (19 miles) south-east of Rome, where Ascanius is said to have moved as founder, supposedly in the twelfth century BC, was a very old settlement. It seems to have headed a league of cities in Latium, retaining its power until the seventh century BC.

The Romans looked on Romulus as their first king (his name is clearly from the same root as *Roma*). The wolf and twins story, the rival augury at the foundation of Rome, the killing of Remus, the setting up of an *asylum* (refugee area) on an approach to the Capitol—these were hallowed myths perhaps far removed from historical truth. The deification of Romulus, who became Quirinus after his mysterious ascension, sounds like a Greek type of myth. The Romans of the late Republic and Empire had little to refer to if they were interested in the earliest period of their history, having no written records and hardly any buildings left from it. Scholars like Varro, whose *Antiquities* in forty-one books (47 BC; only fragments survive) had enormous influence, were partly building on guesswork. In some spheres the modern archaeologist is able to make quite as substantial a contribution as the ancient literary evidence.

## THE TRIBES OF ITALY

Italy was inhabited by many different tribes. They are thought to have migrated from the north and north-east, and a long time before Rome comes into the historical picture we find almost the whole peninsula peopled by them. The so-called Villanovan culture, named after a town near Bologna where the first Iron Age cemetery was investigated, dates from the tenth or ninth century BC onwards. The hilly central areas of Italy came to be inhabited among others by Sabelli, Umbrians and Volsci. Sabelli, who spoke Oscan, were not a tribe but the Latin name for a group of tribes: Apulians, Campanians, Lucanians, Sabines (who provided the best-known women in Roman historical legend), Samnites and others. The areas to which they did not penetrate or from which they were ejected were Etruria on the west coast, where the Etruscans were strongly entrenched, and the Greek maritime colonies of the south and the Naples area. The oldest of these was Cumae, near the Gulf of Naples, a sulphur-gas zone associated in mythology with the Sibyl and the underworld. Nearby Naples (despite its name Neapolis = new city), Pompeii and Paestum were also ancient foundations. In the south, the most flourishing after the early period was Tarentum (Taranto), which originated as the only colony of Sparta. Greek colonies had an enormous influence on the development of Roman culture. The cross-fertilisation of these colonists and Latins almost certainly developed the Latin alphabet, and later it gave Rome her first literary figure, Livius Andronicus.

The early history of Rome is closely bound up with Etruria, and the Romans must have learnt much from this unusual and gifted people. Whereas the Italian tribes, including Latins, spoke Italic dialects, all of them Indo-European and to some extent mutually intelligible, the Etruscan language is totally different. The Greek alphabet was borrowed from the Phoenician, while the Etruscan alphabet is an adaptation of a Greek alphabet used at Cumae; but Etruscan is a non-Indo-European language. About 10,000 mostly short texts, many of them epitaphs or prayers, survive, and progress is being made in deciphering them.

The Etruscans were regarded by some ancient writers as having migrated from Asia Minor, by others as indigenous, while modern opinion is divided. They occupied a territory roughly corresponding to modern Tuscany, and for a time expanded northwards into the Po valley and southwards to Capua. At Spina, a port near one mouth of the Po founded in the sixth century BC, Greeks and Etruscans seem to have lived side by side. Frescoes from Tarquinii and elsewhere show on the one hand scenes of dancing, feasting and hunting, on the other a deep preoccupation with death and with the powers of the underworld.

### THE PERIOD OF THE KINGS

There can be no doubt that during at least part of the regal period Rome was very closely associated with the Etruscans. Since a name which is certainly Etruscan is said to be that of the fifth and seventh (last) kings, Tarquin the Elder and Tarquin the Proud, Etruscan influence was probably strongest during that period. The chief debts of Rome to the Etruscans were in religion, acting, art and architecture, surveying and engineering. In addition to the splendid achievements of Etruscan art, the visitor to Etruria should look at what little remains of their drainage works. One can trace a number of links between religion and early surveying, including the directions faced by augurs looking for favourable or unfavourable signs and surveyors taking their bearings, as well as some of the technical terms.

To King Numa, whose name is Etruscan but who is generally said to have come from the Sabine country, are ascribed the institution of colleges of priests and a reform of the calendar, which as always in early communities had strong religious connections. The sixth king, Servius Tullius, is credited with having set up a political assembly organised on a military basis. It is said to have had eighteen 'centuries' (groups originally 100 strong) of cavalry, 170 of infantry, divided into five classes according to wealth and subdivided into *seniores*, aged 46–60, and *iuniores*, 17–45.

Some light is thrown on the workings of a federation in this early age. Roman tradition, as recorded by Livy, makes the second Tarquin a despotic king who tried to lord it over the Latin league. It was the custom in that league that the member states should discuss policy as equals, and they resented being dominated by an Etruscan-born king. We can ignore the immediate cause of his downfall, while admitting that if there were scandals in the royal family this haughty behaviour towards allies would make the monarchy all the more vulnerable. The traditional date of the founding of the Republic is 509 BC; some modern historians would place it later.

This chapter takes us from legend to fact. There can be little doubt that kings held sway in Rome, which was then a very small settlement grouped round the Capitoline and Palatine hills. An inscription (Fig 2) which seems to be important confirmation of this contains the word *rex*, 'king'.

Fig 2    Inscription on a sherd found near the Regia in the forum at Rome

# 2

# *How a City Grew into an Empire*

WHEN the kings were expelled and Rome became a republic, Etruscan interests became less dominant. A treaty of the early fifth century BC between Rome and a federation of eight Latin cities laid the foundation for a steady development of Roman control. In 396 BC the strong Etruscan settlement of Veii, only 14km (9 miles) north of Rome, was captured by the Romans. A horde of Gauls sacked Rome a few years later, but were eventually bought off with gold. Perhaps no less serious a struggle was the internal one between patricians and plebeians, which after constant disputes and 'secessions', ie withdrawals, led to an eventual settlement which was fair to the plebs.

In 494 BC, according to Livy, Menenius Agrippa, who was sent by the plebeians on the Aventine to the Senate, used a parable to describe the position of the plebs: once upon a time the other parts of the body objected to having to provide all food and drink for the stomach, which had nothing to do but enjoy it, so they went on strike. This resulted in the whole body being terribly weakened, so that the contributions of both stomach and other parts became obvious! The last secession was in 298 BC, when the plebs decamped to the Janiculum and the Senate was forced to give up vetoing *plebiscita*, resolutions of the plebs.

About 360 BC the Romans gained a dominant position in the Latin league, and by 338 their control of central Italy was complete. Their defeat of the Samnites (290) brought them into conflict with the Greek colonies of southern Italy and with King Pyrrhus of Epirus. Success against these opponents made them an international power, as is shown by a treaty with Egypt in 273, establishing diplomatic relations.


### THE ARMY

At this time the Roman army was a citizen militia, raised as and when required from men of military age (17–60) who had a certain minimum amount of property or money. The largest unit was the legion, each legion numbering 5,000 infantry and 300 cavalry. The commanders were the consuls, supported by military tribunes. On the field of battle the legion was customarily drawn up in three lines of soldiers, *hastati* and *principes* in looser formation in front, *triarii* leading a closer-packed rear formation. If the young *hastati* and experienced *principes* had to fall back, the older *triarii* would withstand an attack. In width, each line perhaps consisted of fifteen *manipuli*, groups of about sixty to seventy men each (fewer, larger groups came later). The size of their army varied considerably. The looser Roman formation proved superior to the solid triangular battle unit of the Macedonian and other Greek armies, and in organisation and formation to such other ancient army units as are recorded.


### THE PUNIC WARS AND
### CONTROL OF THE MEDITERRANEAN

But an army alone was not enough to ensure Roman expansion. In 264 BC Rome had to learn the use of sea power, turning sea fights into something like land fights by the invention of the grappling-hook, which enabled their soldiers to board enemy vessels. The greatest naval and commercial power in the western Mediterranean was Carthage, founded by Phoenicians about 800 or 750 BC. For most of sixty years Carthaginians were to challenge Roman power, and in one raid even reached within 3 miles of Rome. The Carthaginians had established themselves in west Sicily, while east Sicily was mostly dominated by the Greek colony of Syracuse. In Messana (Messina) a group of Mamertines, mercenary soldiers whose name means 'men of Mars', had infiltrated from Campania and seized power. Beseiged by King Hiero of Syracuse, they first called in a Carthaginian admiral, then asked for help from Rome. This led to the First Punic War, conducted both by land and sea, which lasted until 241, when Rome forced the Carthaginians out of Sicily and also extracted war reparations.

To secure their position in the North, when in 225 BC Gallic tribes invaded Etruria, the Romans decided to annex all northern Italy south of the Po valley. But meanwhile the Carthaginians too were moving northwards, into the hinterland of Spain, where their command went in 221 to Hannibal, aged twenty-five and son of Hamilcar, a general of the First Punic War. Saguntum, on the east coast of Spain, had a defence alliance with Rome, and when besieged by Hannibal, called for help. Rome sent a deputation to protest, but only when Hannibal had captured the town (219) did they take more positive action.

The following year the Second Punic War started, and the Romans suffered large-scale invasion of their lands when Hannibal crossed the Alps and won the battles of the Trebia and Lake Trasimene. On the defensive, Rome adopted harrying tactics somewhat akin to guerrilla warfare. This policy, known as 'Fabian' from her general Q. Fabius Maximus, was interrupted only by the pitched battle near Cannae (216), where a Roman army of over 50,000 was almost obliterated. Yet Rome, fighting on her own soil or that of her allies, had the advantage over the strained resources of a power far from its base on another continent. Syracuse was captured; Hannibal's bases at Capua and Tarentum, which he had taken in 216 and 213, were won back in 211 and 209; and his brother Hasdrubal, who marched from Spain with reinforcements, was beaten and killed at the battle of the Metaurus (207). The war ended when Rome, with an army and fleet under Scipio Africanus, invaded the Carthaginian homeland of North Africa (204–202). Carthage surrendered Spain, and acknowledged Rome's overlordship, but the Romans evacuated Africa.

One of Hannibal's allies, though inactive, was Macedon, and in 197 the Romans under Flamininus defeated King Philip V of Macedon at Cynoscephalae. By this and by the battle of Pydna in 168 they gained control of Macedon and mainland Greece.

The years 146 and 133 BC both witnessed Roman expansion in the West and East simultaneously. In 146 Carthage and Corinth were destroyed; Cato had feared Carthage as an economic and possibly military rival and ended every speech 'Carthage must be destroyed'. In 133 the hill-fort of Numantia in north Spain was captured, a key post in a long war; and expansion in Asia Minor was facilitated by the fact that Attalus III of Pergamum, clearly fearing a revolutionary party, bequeathed his kingdom to Rome. Figure 3 shows the dates of

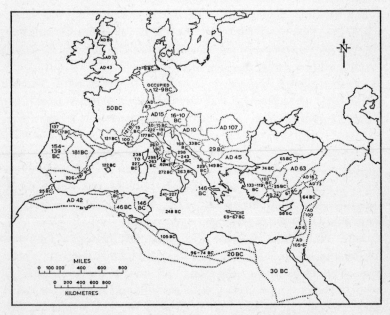

Fig 3    The extent of Rome's sphere of influence

acquisition or of an alliance of territories under Rome. Germany was abandoned after the defeat of P. Quinctilius Varus in AD 9.

## PROBLEMS UNDER THE LATE REPUBLIC

Rapid growth of territory brought problems, when wealthy men defied the rule that such conquered territories as were designated *ager publicus* (public land) should be worked by small-holders. In 133 Tiberius Gracchus, a tribune of the people, sounded a note of alarm over the growth of the large estates and lack of small-holders (potentially military manpower) in Etruria and Sicily; in the latter (p 55) slaves had revolted. He declared his determination to limit holdings (as described in Chapter 6), but his death by violence slowed down his supporters' plans. His younger brother Gaius Gracchus, tribune in 123 and 122 BC, supplemented Tiberius' reform by founding colonies of small-holders in Italy and one at Carthage. When he proposed to extend citizenship, however, another important corollary of territorial expansion, rioting in Rome and appalling bloodshed ensued (121).

In the last years of the second century BC Jugurtha, king of Numidia, who since 111 had been at war with Rome, met his match in C. Marius, a native of the Arpinum area who had fought well at Numantia and was successful in Africa with a divide-and-rule policy. Despite senate opposition, Marius had raised an army from the poorest citizens: legionary service was actually regarded as a privilege, so that this extension of qualification brought in many keen men loyal to their commander.

On the northern front a vast horde of Cimbri and Teutones from Jutland and Frisia had slaughtered a Roman army near Arausio (Orange) in 105, and fear prompted the election of Marius as consul for five years in succession (104–100). He trained another army, and was probably responsible for replacing the old three battle lines by a cohort formation (ten cohorts to each legion). In 102 he defeated the Teutones near Aquae Sextiae (Aix-en-Provence), and the next year he and Q. Lutatius Catulus were victorious over the Cimbri near Vercellae (Vercelli, North Italy).

The domination of large continental areas by one city, which is difficult for people in this century to understand, had created great internal weaknesses. The Roman Senate's decision in 91 BC that a proposal to give all Italians full Roman citizenship was unconstitutional infuriated the Italians. The following year they actually set up a rival capital, 'Italia', at Corfinium, and this had the desired effect. The citizenship was granted and the war came to an end. Although the voting power of the Italians remained limited because they were registered in a minority of tribes (Chapter 3), still from this time one can think in terms of what we might call a country rather than a city alone. All these areas had a great deal of similarity of terrain, with steep slopes which often needed terracing for cultivation, and which made land communication a challenge, a challenge however that the Romans could meet. Climatically the Mediterranean type was still predominant, and familiar crops flourished.

But the Romans were beginning to push into desert areas in the south and east and cooler areas in the north and west. Moreover in these latter regions the people had less history of civilisation. Wars continued on the outer frontiers, eg Asia Minor and Spain, and from time to time there were rebellions in Italy, caused by consuls' struggles for absolute power, the most conspicuous being Sulla, who used such power from 82 to 79 to reinstate the authority of the Senate, which had been weakened by Marius' party.

Two major crises at home were the Spartacus slave revolt (73–71) and the Catilinarian conspiracy (63), dealt with initially by legislation. Catiline (L. Sergius Catilina) was an impoverished patrician who advocated cancellation of debts. After an earlier unsuccessful attempt, he formed a conspiracy to distract the authorities with rioting and arson while he marched on Rome with an army from Etruria. Cicero learnt of the plot from envoys of a Gallic tribe, passed emergency legislation and executed Catiline's supporters in Rome, after which their leader was killed in battle.

Expansion had been vigorously effected by the army, but new territories had to be governed and their economies developed. It began to look as though the existing Republican constitution was not adequate to cope with all government at home and outside Italy. The man who brought about the downfall of the Republic was Julius Caesar. A champion of the *populares*, lavishing money beyond his means and already Pontifex Maximus (p 57), he joined forces in 59 with Pompey and Crassus. They formed an unofficial Triumvirate. In this, Pompey was the top soldier of the day, with military experience gained in several provinces and a wide support among the legions, Crassus the leading financier, and Caesar himself the most enterprising populist politician. Caesar used the alliance to turn himself into a soldier as well. He was given charge of Cisalpine Gaul and Illyria, and later of Narbonese Gaul. Highly successful in Gaul, where fresh migrations were threatening, he twice penetrated Britain (55 and 54 BC). In Gaul the lack of complete mountain barriers enabled him to advance rapidly, but also permitted the barbarians to pour southwards from north and central Europe as well as from offshore islands. He treated certain tribes mercilessly, and the younger Cato and others in Rome demanded he should be handed over in chains to them. To prevent or postpone this, he wanted permission to stand for the consulship in his absence, but the Senate, with Pompey's support, refused the request. This led to civil war and the defeat of Pompey by Caesar at the battle of Pharsalia (near Farsala, Greece) in 48 BC and of most of his followers by 45. Caesar pardoned nearly all his enemies, assumed a dictatorship and reorganised much of the administration. So the stage was set for an imperial system, with strong government from the capital city, Rome.

As its population had grown so much, Caesar reduced the numbers receiving free corn and settled 80,000 in new overseas colonies, thus ensuring a human barrier, with vested interests in the land, against barbarians. He incorporated Cisalpine Gaul into Italy, reduced the burden of taxation in the provinces, and admitted to Roman citizenship, among others, all the members of a legion he had recruited in Gaul. He reformed local government and the calendar, and started planning an expedition against Parthia. His assassination by Brutus and Cassius (44) came at a time when he had assumed more and more powers and showed contempt for the slowness of democratic processes.

The ensuing struggle for power resulted in control by an official Second Triumvirate, of Caesar's right-hand man Mark Antony, his young great-nephew and adopted son Octavian, and his senatorial champion Lepidus. They put to death many opponents, including Cicero, confiscated lands for their veterans, and defeated Brutus and Cassius at Philippi (42). A division of provinces (Fig 3) gave Antony the East, Octavian the West, and led to a further civil war in which Octavian defeated Antony and Cleopatra, queen of Egypt, at the sea battle off Actium, West Greece (31).

### IMPERIAL CONSOLIDATION AND EXPANSION

Augustus (a name conveying an aura of reverence), as Octavian now liked to be known, proved skilful at preserving the semblance of the Republican constitution while effectively concentrating power on himself. The actual title Augustus was conferred on him by the Senate in 27 BC at his suggestion, when they persuaded him not to resign. He reduced the numbers of the Senate, but shared the rule to some extent with it, placing only the less peaceful provinces under his direct rule, but from 23 BC he wielded an overall control even over senatorial provinces. The army was made to look to him as its head, just as Caesar's legions had venerated *him* in the Gallic and Civil Wars. It now became a permanent army composed of legionaries, who were Roman citizens, and auxiliary forces, given citizenship on completion of service. The length of service was at first sixteen years plus four as veteran, then twenty plus five (twenty-five plus five in the second century). During their non-veteran service, legionaries were not allowed to contract official marriages. As a bodyguard and home force Augustus instituted the Praetorian Guard. Much of his work was constructive after the ruin and neglect caused by the civil wars: new colonies, new buildings, restoration of temples, organisation of public services, social legislation etc. For forty years he was *princeps*, 'leading man', *imperator*, 'military commander' (the word from which 'emperor' is derived), and *pater patriae*, 'father of the fatherland', and he planned to pass this power, strengthened by an imperial cult and deification of deceased emperors, on to his grandsons. But first his favourite nephew, then the grandsons died, so that finally he adopted his stepson Tiberius as successor, and the concept of a family succession was established. On the military front Augustus' principate had shown some losses on outer frontiers, particularly in the Teutoburg Forest, Germany, but in general it was a period of peace and stabilisation.

Tiberius, who had helped to rescue the situation on the northern frontier, took over the principate unwillingly but with a strong sense of duty to Augustus. He was intent on keeping the Empire the same size as it had been under his predecessor, and succeeded. Claudius, the next emperor but one, maligned by certain wits for his ponderous scholarship and his unattractive physical handicap (a limp and a continual slobber), had become an historian before the Praetorians insisted on his becoming emperor. In AD 43 he organised and took part in the expedition under A. Plautius Silvanus which extended the boundaries of the Empire and won Britain as a province.

The Roman occupation of Britain lasted from then to AD 410. In the early stages there was little opposition. There were, in fact, friendly chieftains, including Tiberius Claudius Cogidubnus, who was recognised as king and *legatus* of the emperor in south central Britain. It seems likely that the imposing palace at Fishbourne, near Chichester, was his. Camulodunum

(Colchester), immediately after its capture, became the base for the expedition, but London was soon chosen as the capital. Under Septimius Severus Britain was divided into two provinces, with capitals at London and York, and later into four. The colony at Colchester and the Roman settlements at Verulamium (St Albans) and London were sacked by Boudicca in AD 60, but order was restored by Suetonius Paulinus. Wales was subdued by Frontinus and northern England and the lowlands of Scotland by Agricola.

To some extent the success and stability of the Empire was dependent on the personality of its emperor. Nero became notorious for his handling of the Great Fire of Rome (64), for his ill-treatment of Christians, who were blamed for it, and for his wasteful artistic quirks. There were revolts both at home and in the provinces, including Britain as mentioned above. The outcome of dissatisfaction and a series of conspiracies was civil war and the 'year of the four emperors', with settled conditions only when Vespasian was acclaimed emperor.

Vespasian had distinguished himself in army service in Britain and Judaea. He was a countryman, blunt, superstitious, hard-working (he started work before dawn) and efficient. Since the death of Nero, the emperors had not been connected with the family of the Caesars; but Vespasian was able to build up his own dynasty, the Flavian. His greatest contribution was the placing of the State revenues and the economy of the Empire on a sound footing once more. According to Suetonius he let it be known that 40,000 million sesterces, a stupendous sum, were needed to stabilise the economy, and he duly set about raising them. The sum has been doubted; but viewed as capital it might be correct. The annual revenue from Egypt at this time was over 500 million sesterces.

Under the sway of Vespasian's younger son, Domitian, the principate became an even more tyrannical institution than before. Domitian insisted on being addressed 'lord and god', and probably killed off more possible opponents than any previous emperor. His administration was sound enough, but he failed to secure one frontier by recalling Agricola, who, while campaigning in Britain from 78 to 83, had realised the strategic desirability of subduing Ireland and the Highlands of Scotland. By making the sea the frontier, this might have proved safer and cheaper in the long run. Domitian, however, decided otherwise, with lasting consequences for the future of the British Isles.

Sixteen months after Domitian's assassination Trajan, a Spaniard by birth, became emperor. His main contributions were the securing of the northern frontier and the organisation of public works. His sculptured column in Rome shows scenes from his Dacian wars (101–105), which resulted in the annexation of Dacia. Romanisation was so firmly implanted in that province that the people still speak a Latin-descended language, Rumanian. Trajan's correspondence with the younger Pliny over Bithynia shows him as a firm and sensible administrator. Hadrian, his successor and a relative, was a great traveller who toured the Empire observing conditions and co-ordinating Roman rule. The best known of his practical measures is his Wall, designed as a separation of the barbarian tribes to the north from the Romanised Britons to the south. Made of stone in the east and turf in the west, it was 5m (15ft) high and 122km (76 miles) long. Pons Aelius (Newcastle upon Tyne), was named after him (P. Aelius Hadrianus), as was the Roman colony planted at Jerusalem. Antoninus Pius, the next emperor, was also of an originally provincial family, from Nîmes. He too continued to try to control northern Britain, building a wall, the Antonine Wall, against the people of the Highlands. He centralised and strengthened the civil service and left the treasury in a strong position. The Empire was now at its fullest geographical extent and enjoying its longest period of political stability.

### THE ROMANS AND OTHER RACES

Who, then, were the Romans? In the wider sense they eventually included a whole empire of types with a vast population (Table 1), from negroes and North Africans to Asiatics and a complete range of what we know today as Europeans. To the Greek, barbarian meant non-Greek; to the Roman, at least after the time of Plautus, for whom translating into barbarian language meant translating into Latin, it stood for anyone outside the greater Greek and Roman worlds combined. There was never any doubt in the mind of a Roman that the great majority of barbarians were inferior, even if worthwhile tips could be learnt from them. The only doubt came when Romans tried to assess their own civilisation in comparison with that of Greek cities. Here we find from time to time an inferiority complex, a strong desire to claim that Rome is able to equal or even to outrival Greece in various spheres.

Although Latin and Greek were the only widely used languages, in the provinces there was a variety of local languages as well, eg Punic in North Africa, Celtic in Gaul and elsewhere. The influx into Rome of professional men, merchants and slaves from outside Italy was enormous. These soon learnt Latin, but only Greek speakers were keen to keep up their own language, which throughout the Roman period was respected as a source of education and culture.

The Romans of Rome, like many of their neighbours, were a mostly small and dark-haired race. Roman writers express astonishment at the great height and fair hair of so many members of the German tribes. We possess numerous statues of Roman men and women and coins of magistrates and emperors from which we can build up a good idea of physical features. Some of these are idealised, but in some the artist has delighted in showing very plain faces or even physical deformities. Often a man's head is on the small side, the hair thin on top, the ears protruding. The Roman nose, straight and sometimes large, is a noticeable feature of a good percentage of the men and women. As one might expect, the excessively fat Roman tends to be a wealthy man under the Empire.

## TABLE 1     POPULATION

### 1 *Census Statistics of Roman Citizens*

| Date | Number of Citizens |
|---|---|
| 131–130 BC | 318,823 |
| 125–124 BC | 394,736 |
| 115–114 BC | 394,336 |
| 86–85 BC | 463,000 |
| 70–69 BC | 910,000 |
| 28 BC | 4,063,000 |
| 8 BC | 4,233,000 |
| AD 14 | 4,937,000 |
| AD 47 | 5,984,072 |

### 2 *Regions of the Empire in AD 14 (estimates)*

| | |
|---|---|
| Italy including Rome | 13,000,000 (see note 1) |
| Sicily, Sardinia, Corsica | 1,100,000 |
| Spain | 6,000,000 |
| Gaul | 4,900,000 |
| Danube provinces | 2,000,000 |
| Greek mainland and islands | 3,000,000 |
| Asia Minor | 13,000,000 |
| Syria, Palestine, Cyprus | 6,500,000 |
| Egypt, Cyrenaica | 5,500,000 |
| Remainder of North Africa | 6,000,000 |
| Total | 61,000,000 |

### 3 *City of Rome (estimates)*

| Date | Free men and boys over 10 years | Total | Area | Density |
|---|---|---|---|---|
| 5 BC | 320,000 | c 900,000 | 1,245 ha (3,075 acres) | c 723 per ha (c 293 per acre) |
| c AD 200 | ? | 800,000– 1 million | 1,245 ha (3,075 acres) | 642–803 per ha (260–325 per acre) |

4 *Some Principal Cities* (*mainly estimates*)

| | | |
|---|---|---|
| Rome | 5 BC | c 900,000 |
| Alexandria | 50 BC | Over 300,000 free (Diodorus) |
| Carthage | Fourth century AD | c 400,000 free (Herodian, Ausonius) |
| Antioch | First century BC, fourth century AD | c 300,000 free (Strabo, Ausonius) |
| Pergamum | Second century AD | c 180,000 total (Galen) |
| Ephesus | Second to third century AD | c 180,000 total (inscription) |
| Apamea, Syria | First century BC–AD | 117,000 free; census included extensive territory |

NOTES

1 Ancient census figures relate only to Roman citizens, ie excluding women, children, foreigners and slaves. A more complete estimate of population can be made by multiplying by 4–4½. Citizenship was extended in 89 BC, and the full effects of this were appreciated by 70 BC. There were losses of life during the civil wars, yet the number of citizens was multiplied 4½ times between 69 and 28 BC: in 49 BC Cisalpine Gaul was included in Italy, and after the civil wars at least 108 colonies were founded, but the vast increase may indicate that until 28 BC the censors had not included citizens in colonies or outside Italy. The figure for AD 14 may represent about 3 million (or even more) citizens in Italy, including Rome, the remainder (an admittedly high figure) being outside Italy. The figure for AD 47 is Tacitus'; others give about 6,900,000. Several scholars have suggested that the figures from 28 BC onwards include wives and children of citizens; but this seems unlikely in view of Augustus' words *civium Romanorum capita*, literally 'heads of Roman citizens'.

2 The figures given by K. J. Beloch, writing between 1886 and 1906, are: Italy including Rome, 6–8 million; Sicily, 600,000; other areas as given here. For recent research see

P. A. Brunt, *Italian Manpower, 225 BC–AD 14* (Oxford, 1971);
R. P. Duncan-Jones, *The Economy of the Roman Empire* (Cambridge, 1974). The figure for Rome including Italy is that of
Nissen, 10 million free inhabitants, plus 3 million slaves. The
total for free inhabitants may be compared with the estimate of
3 million citizens (adult males) suggested in note 1.

3 The first estimate is based on Augustus' gratuity of 60
denarii a head (thought to have been paid to men and boys
over ten years of age). This figure is a compromise between the
750,000 estimate of P. A. Brunt, op cit, and an earlier estimate
of 1,200,000. The second reflects the city's wheat consumption
—27,375,000 *modii*, c 239,000cu m.

4 Figures in this section are very approximate except for the
free populations of Pergamum and Apamea.

## THE GEOGRAPHY OF THE ROMAN WORLD

The geographical variations increased as Rome spread into
wider and wider areas. The degree of control of or adaptation
to environment was a vital factor in expansion and government
of territories. The most completely Roman way of life, not
surprisingly, did tend to succeed and persist where the olive and
the vine grew; but this fact must be related to greater proximity
to Rome as well as to climate.

Rome is roughly halfway from north to south of the Italian
peninsula, which is about 1,100km (683 miles) long but at
most 250km (155 miles) wide. The steep-sided Apennines run
the entire length of it and restrict lowland areas to small patches
in river valleys and on coasts. Some of the coastal areas, particularly the Pomptine marshes and the mouths of the Po, were
poorly drained and at times malarial. Much of the hill country
consists of rather porous limestone, which with thin soil and
summer drought is apt to produce poor crops. There are also
volcanic areas: Vesuvius is still active and periodically highly
explosive. These give rise to some very fertile soil. The slopes
everywhere required terracing to hold the soil, still an important feature of husbandry. The warm sunny climate was and

is particularly good for the growing of vines and olives. The relief encouraged fragmentation, and a city-state like Rome was only able to conquer and unite the tribes by her skill in building land communications, especially across the steep Apennine ridges.

In ancient times fishing off the coasts was very productive. The river mouths offer better harbours on the west than the east coast of central Italy. Both Rome itself and Ostia at the mouth of the Tiber were ports, the former for vessels of limited draught. As Rome's domain increased, she was also able to use, for example, ports on the Gulf of Naples, such as Puteoli (Pozzuoli), a town subject then, as today, to earthquakes and changes of coastline. Rivers, such as the Arno, which cannot now be navigated were navigable in ancient times. Areas of southern Italy, such as Metaponto, which are now developing after long being poverty-stricken, were amongst the most fertile and prosperous. Campania was densely settled, good farming land and a favourite area for summer villas. The flat Po valley, which was incorporated into Italy in 42 BC, had been drained even before the Roman occupation, by the Etruscans, except near the Adriatic, where the land was even more marshy than today. Drainage was carried out in connection with the building of the Via Aemilia in 187 BC, and from the numbers of colonists sent out by Rome (eg 6,000 each at Cremona and Placentia in 219 BC) it can be seen that the area came to be comparatively thickly populated.

---

A Campanian coastal scene with villas. Fresco from Stabiae (Castellammare di Stabia), AD 50–60, now in Naples.

Corn-measuring at Ostia harbour. Mosaic, c AD 112, in the 'Aula dei Mensores', Ostia. The corn-measurer has his left hand on a *modius* filling with corn; in his right hand he holds a cylindrical tally, evidently wooden with holes in it, on which to record the amounts. Two slaves are about to remove the grain in the *modius*, while another brings a further bag of corn. Inscription mutilated and disputed.

At the mid-point of the central peninsula in the Mediterranean, the Romans were well placed to make it *Mare Nostrum*, 'our sea'. Of the islands in the western Mediterranean, only Sicily, which has volcanic deposits caused by eruptions of Etna, had very fertile and thickly populated areas. The Iberian peninsula and the Balkans, with their high mountain ranges and much porous rock, made for isolated units of settlement and presented problems of communication. In Spain the rebel Q. Sertorius was able to harry Roman lines of communication and then quickly retreat into the mountains (80–73 or 72 BC). On the other hand, in many of the lower areas of the Iberian peninsula, especially near the coast and in the southern valleys, agriculture was thriving, and Roman civilisation and the Latin language spread rapidly. In Asia Minor the Greek settlements, especially on and near parts of the western and southern coasts, became busy commercial centres: one such was Ephesus, familiar from the Acts of the Apostles.

The Alps, Pyrenees and Illyrian Alps presented a greater barrier than today. They were regarded not as picturesque playgrounds, as in the modern tourist era, but as fierce natural obstacles. The Romans succeeded in making roads over the Alps, but these were closed for much of the winter. The country to the north of the Alps was more heavily forested than today.

---

Goatherd milking goat. Relief on side of a sarcophagus in Rome.

Cutler's shop. Monument erected by the cutler L. Cornelius Atimetus, first century AD (Vatican Museum). In addition to knives the cutler (*right*), a Greek freedman, sells sickles and other implements. He wears a tunic, while his customer wears a toga.

The main route then from Italy to southern Gaul, south of the Ligurian Alps, was not on coastal corniches and through tunnels, but by an upper route.

The Rhine and Danube line became the most lasting northern limit of penetration, perhaps not so much because it was a physical barrier (bridge-building techniques were excellent) but because of the human and climatic problems involved and the extended lines of communication with Rome. The areas outside the Mediterranean world seemed remote and full of unknown dangers. The concept of an Ocean encircling a more or less circular land mass consisting of Europe, Asia and Africa died hard. Opinions varied whether there was a habitable southern temperate zone, and travellers' stories about weird and wonderful tribes, like the Sciapodes, who used one foot to serve as a sunshade, were commonly believed. In North Africa the Romans encountered a parched land subject to encroachment by the sand. Moreover a large area of the south central Mediterranean was dangerous to navigation owing to sandbank hazards of the Greater and Lesser Syrtes. By digging deep wells and by constant irrigation the Romans were able to make regions fertile which are desert today. But no doubt political stability and continuous attention were required, and there is evidence that about the third century AD the sand was beginning to encroach seriously on the large estates which produced corn for the Roman market. The great oasis and main zone of cultivation, as always, was Egypt, watered by the regular annual Nile floods. Rainfall records kept there by Ptolemy in the second century AD do not show much variation from today in the number of rainy days.

Difficulties of climate were encountered elsewhere too. In Asia Minor the dry plateaux of the interior, with great extremes of temperature, were also a barrier to much settlement. Further south there were droughts, which often led to famine: one such is recorded in Palestine during Claudius' principate. Ovid protests bitterly at the cold winters of Tomis on the north shore of the Black Sea. The climate of Britain was heartily disliked by all who wrote about it in antiquity: fog is what predominates in descriptions. The Channel crossing had no continuous or reliable period of calm and so presented more problems of transport than land areas.

Over the long period of Roman domination wetter and cooler periods occurred in Italy, especially one at the end of the third and beginning of the second century BC. Those accustomed to the generally warm climate of Italy protested far more at cold, damp conditions than at hot, dry ones.

The ancient Romans were nevertheless critical of the climate of their own city. The summer months tend to be very hot. In August and even September those who could afford it usually aimed at going to the countryside or seaside. The great heat breaks with autumn thunderstorms. The winter is short, but has cold and wet spells, with an average of ten to twelve rainy days a month. Between the winter, rainy episodes are mild spells, like good British spring weather, which are a major period for growing. Snow is practically unknown in Rome, though plenty falls on the Apennines and could be a barrier to movement. It is significant that wars usually ceased in winter. During the winter and early spring a cold dry north or NNE wind frequently blows. At all seasons there is a great deal of sunshine, yet there is little twilight at any period of the year. The number of daylight hours varies from over nine at midwinter to under fifteen at midsummer; but the Romans counted twelve hours from sunrise to sunset, whatever the season, so that a Roman hour varied in Rome from about $\frac{3}{4}$ to about $1\frac{1}{4}$ the duration of ours. Since each Roman hour was one-twelfth of the daylight period, there was more difference between length of hours at midsummer and midwinter the further north one went. The comparison in Figure 4 is between Rome, latitude 41° 54', and London, latitude 51° 31'.

An effect of the sunny climate on the people of Rome was to induce them to design their buildings mainly to provide against the heat. Like the Greeks, they transacted much of their business out of doors, partly in shaded porticoes. They also aimed, at least in hot weather, at curtailing the number of working hours. Frequently religious holidays helped to avoid exhaustion in the hotter months, and schools, as today, did not operate in the summer.

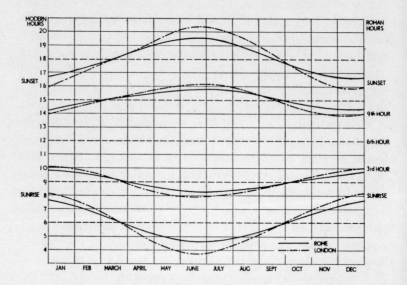

Fig 4    Comparison of Roman and modern hours

# 3

# *How They Organised Their World*

THE Romans had a highly structured system of political government, which evolved from absolute monarchy through a somewhat revolutionary period to a republic, where an elected
government and citizen power were at their zenith. But this
did not last and an imperial structure followed. Under this last
system, the relative political importance of the emperor and
others varied enormously with personalities.

### SENATE AND MAGISTRATES

The body which administered, or appointed men to ad-
minister, the affairs of Rome and its territories, which declared
war and made treaties, which promoted legislation or recommended bills to the popular assemblies, was the Senate (*senatus*).
Its power was at its height, though challenged, during the early
Republic. It was weakened during the late Republic, and very
considerably diminished under the Empire. The growth of
Rome and of her empire made it increasingly difficult for an
intimate type of government, by democracy or discussion, to
operate efficiently.

The members of the Senate were addressed as *patres con-
scripti*, which is often translated 'conscript fathers'; but there
are good grounds for believing that in origin the two words
represented two categories, 'fathers' (heads of patrician families)
and 'enrolled members'. By the time of the late Republic the
distinction between patricians and plebeians had virtually

disappeared, except that patricians were not allowed to become tribunes of the people (*plebs*). The numbers of the Senate, which had fallen, mainly owing to senators being killed in the civil wars or proscriptions, were raised by Sulla during his dictatorship (82–79 BC) from 300 to 600. He appointed some of his friends senators and increased the numbers of magistrates. Senators remained members of the Senate for life, and were expected unless they had a legitimate excuse to attend its meetings. These were held very frequently, whenever the consuls summoned members, either in the Curia or in one of several temples. The government of Rome was known as the Senate and people of Rome, *senatus populusque Romanus*, abbreviated SPQR. The descending hierarchy of consuls, praetors, aediles, tribunes, quaestors and (intermittently) censors was known as magistrates, ie office-bearers: as will be seen, only the praetors corresponded at all closely to what is meant today by the term 'magistrate'.

Except in an emergency, when very occasionally a dictator was appointed (after 202 BC the only dictatorships, of a political nature, were those of Sulla and Julius Caesar), the supreme magistrates were the two consuls. They were appointed by election, normally from among those who had been praetors (see below), and held office for one calendar year, which was called after them. They had the right of speaking first in the Senate, and were among the chief initiators of legislation, to the extent that, if a consul said the auspices were unfavourable, theoretically no business could be done. They were accompanied on official business by twelve lictors carrying *fasces*, bundles of rods signifying authority. In an emergency they could be called upon by a 'final decree of the Senate' to take any measures necessary to protect the State. They had the right to levy troops, and any Roman armies operating in Italy were regularly commanded by them. Ex-consuls (*viri consulares*, literally 'consular men') spoke next in order after consuls, and from the first century BC could be sent out to govern the provinces as proconsuls. Every year the Senate appointed proconsuls or propraetors as provincial governors or extended their appointment, which was normally for one year under the Republic. In the provinces governors had *imperium*, military power, and the *fasces* carried by their lictors contained an axe, which symbolised the power to carry out the death sentence.

As we go down the hierarchy, the function of magistrates becomes more specialised. Praetors (literally 'those going before') were probably the supreme magistrates at one early stage, but came to be the next step down from consuls. Their numbers rose from two to four in 227 BC, when Sicily and Sardinia became provinces, to six in 197 BC, when two Spanish provinces had been added, and to eight under Sulla. Their function was at first largely military but came to be mainly judicial. The urban praetor was the chief legal magistrate in Rome, while the second praetor was in charge of foreigners.

The connection of public games with the State religion is shown in the next magistracy. Aediles (from *aedes* = temple) were in charge of games and some religious organisation, of public works and archives, weights and measures, and markets. There were two types, curule and plebeian aediles. Curule aediles, like consuls and praetors, were regarded as of the class of magistracy entitling the holder and his male descendants to call themselves *nobiles*.

The office one below in the sequence had an origin and function very different from the others. Tribunes of the people (*plebs*) numbered ten from a very early date and originated from the disputes between patricians and plebeians. They were champions of the plebeians, so that when P. Clodius, a patrician, wanted to become one in 59 BC, he had to get himself adopted by a plebeian *gens*. Their persons were sacrosanct and inviolable, and anyone acting against this inviolability could be condemned to loss of political rights and his property confiscated to the temple of Ceres. They had power of intercession, and in the late Republic frequently vetoed business in the popular (= people's) assemblies. This led to rioting and murder at the time of the Gracchi (133–122 BC), and Sulla virtually abolished the office, but it was restored in 75 BC and given back its full rights five years later. The inviolability conferred upon the office was so important that emperors were keen to claim tribunician power every year.

The magistrates of lowest rank having an automatic right to be senators were quaestors, whose numbers rose as follows:

| | |
|---|---|
| Monarchy and early Republic | 2 |
| 425 BC (2 treasury officials added) | 4 |
| 267 BC (4 local quaestors added) | 8 |
| At dates of acquisition of the earlier provinces (provincial quaestors added) | 9–19 |
| 81 BC (1 added for water supply) | 20 |
| 46–45 BC (number doubled by Caesar) | 40 |
| c 27 BC (number halved by Augustus) | 20 |

They were financial officers, originally military but branching out into civilian finance first in Rome, then elsewhere: Sicily had two, other provinces one each. The young man who aspired to magistracies (*honores*) started as quaestor and went through some or all of the higher offices to complete his *cursus honorum* (public career structure).

Apart from the magistracies whose holders followed each other without a break, there were two censors appointed by the Senate from its numbers every five years to hold office for eighteen months. Their duties were to conduct a census, to supervise morals, to control the size of the Senate by enrolling members not automatically qualified (in the late Republic, election to the quaestorship was the main qualification) or if necessary expelling members, and to decide who was a member of the equestrian order.

The Senate was by its composition a body likely to be conservative. Most of the consuls of the second and first centuries BC were *nobiles*: one like Cicero who was a *novus homo* (new man, ie non-*nobilis*) was an exception. The Senate and the *equites** were the wealthiest orders, and there was even a monetary qualification: senators were supposed to possess a minimum capital of 1,000,000 sesterces under the late Republic.

*For *equites* see p. 47

### ASSEMBLIES

Popular assemblies were summoned and presided over by the consuls. There were two types of assembly operating in the late Republic. The army had one, the *comitia centuriata*, where voting was by the 'centuries' of seniors and juniors; this assembly gradually acquired political rights. The other, the *comitia tributa*, constituted an assembly either of the plebeians or of all the people, where in either case voting was by tribes. Originally there were three tribes; in the early Republic we find four urban and an increasing number of rural tribes, sixteen of which were called after the patrician families. From 241 BC there were thirty-five tribes, spread over rural areas as well as Rome, and each Roman citizen was allotted to one of them, usually according to the place from which his family came. The functions of both types of popular assembly were the election of magistrates, and the passing or rejecting of *rogationes* (bills) submitted to these bodies; if passed, they became law.

The fact that individual 'centuries' or tribes had power which they could wield by giving their votes to particular candidates led to much canvassing of their prominent members. There was a thinly disguised line between illegal bribery and permitted largesse, such as free banquets. In this type of canvassing the patron-client relationship played a big part. There were never any political parties as such either in the Senate or the popular assemblies, and Republican politics hinged mainly round the names of the leading men at any one time. But towards the end of the Republic a fair number of senators called themselves or were called *optimates* as opposed to others known as *populares*. The first of these groups included very conservative members and more moderate politicians like Cicero, who was keen on a *concordia ordinum*, ie agreement between the senate and *equites*. The second group was more revolutionary and pressed for such measures as land reform and cancellation of personal debts.

## CHANGES UNDER THE EMPIRE

The political system under the Empire evolved from the Republican system, since Augustus liked to appear to preserve the semblance of freer political structure and to carry on the tradition of Julius Caesar, who had been a leader of the *populares*. On the military side Augustus called himself *imperator*, actually as a first name, but otherwise following the Republican practice of so calling a general with *imperium*, military power. Although it is from this word that 'emperor' is derived, from the civilian point of view the regular term was *princeps*, 'leading man', so that it is more correct to speak of a principate than a reign. The word *rex*, 'king', was carefully avoided in reference to emperors, since it recalled the expelled Tarquins.

At first Augustus wielded power by being one of the two consuls each year; there was Republican precedent for this with Marius. Such a system had disadvantages, the chief of which was that the number of ex-consuls, who as proconsuls could be appointed to govern provinces, gradually diminished. So in 23 BC a revised constitution gave Augustus as his principal powers (1) a 'greater proconsular *imperium*', which placed him above proconsuls, and (2) tribunician power. Being of patrician family he could not be a tribune of the *plebs*, but as successor to Julius Caesar he valued the sacrosanctity and veto power of tribunes. Emperors after him were anxious to claim this power annually, and as they regularly enumerated the years of their tribunician power, we have, subject to adjustment, an easy method of reckoning the years of their principate. The Senate continued to function throughout the Empire, sharing the functions of government (but in some cases more as a rubber stamp) with the emperor. For the election of magistrates Augustus operated through powers of nomination or commendation to the popular assemblies (about AD 5 a new regulation provided that consuls and praetors should be designated by ten 'centuries' of Senators and *equites*); but under his successors these assemblies were abolished except for voting tribunician power, and the emperor had direct control of nominations.

### ADMINISTRATION OF TERRITORIES

Government through the Senate and people of Rome included more and more areas and peoples as Rome's territories expanded. From 89 BC Italians were enrolled as Roman citizens and could vote in Rome; yet there was also local government. Towns in Italy were classified as either *municipia* or *coloniae*, and both these terms spread to the provinces.

Under the Republic, *municipia* were not colonies but had alliance agreements with Rome. Their citizens could marry Romans and would become Roman citizens if they went to live in Rome or if the town acquired voting rights. They could enter into legal contracts with Romans without depending on international law. These towns undertook to provide troops for Rome, but for internal administration were allowed free choice, only being visited once a year by Roman prefects to see that all was in order. As a result we find much variation in the local government of such towns. Under the Empire many civilised towns in the provinces were allowed to call themselves *municipia* or *coloniae*. In either group, both in Italy and the provinces, a body of ex-magistrates known as the *decuriones* organised much of the routine administration.

The word 'colony' is regularly used for *coloniae*, but these were totally different from colonies of European powers. The name means settlements of *coloni*, small-holders, either for defence or to promote agriculture or both. They were often intended in the first instance as places where veterans, ie retired legionaries, could be rewarded by an allocation of land. The earliest, dating to the fourth century BC, were all on the coast: Ostia, Antium (Anzio), and Tarracina (Terracina). As Roman territory expanded, allocations grew and colonies were founded farther away: in the second century BC especially in the Po valley, and after the destruction of Carthage (146 BC) in North Africa. In Britain colonies were established at Colchester, Lincoln, Gloucester and subsequently York. The administration of colonies tended to be based on the pattern of Rome's; thus they were led by *duoviri* who corresponded to the two consuls.

The term *provincia*, province, literally meant a sphere of action of a magistrate who had *imperium*. Since the spheres of action outside Italy were allocated annually by the Senate on a territorial basis, the word came to be used for a specific territory outside Italy. The first two were Sicily (227 BC, extending to Syracuse 211 BC) and Sardinia (227). After some years a praetor was appointed to look after each of these, and two for Spain. However, with a change of policy from 146 BC, the new provinces of Africa, Macedonia and others were annexed, and governors were appointed from ex-magistrates, ie proconsuls and propraetors. If necessary their command was extended beyond one year, or in an emergency provinces could be combined under one man's command. Subject to the foundation charter, the governor was allowed a very free hand, which produced unscrupulous men like C. Verres, governor of Sicily 73–71 BC, who fleeced the population wholesale to make his own fortune.

Under Augustus the provinces were divided between himself and the Senate, in such a way that he through his nominees administered the more warlike ones, while the Senate retained control, subject to the possibility of his interference, of the more peaceful. The introduction by Augustus of salaries for provincial administrators helped to lessen cases of extortion. From literary sources we know something of Cn. Iulius Agricola, father-in-law of Tacitus and governor of Britain AD 78–84, and more from the letters of the younger Pliny, who shows constant preoccupation with justice and efficiency in his area of Asia Minor. Diocletian doubled the number of provinces by dividing them, put *equites* in charge of them, and grouped them into twelve dioceses (civic, not religious), with a *vicarius* in charge of each.

### SOCIAL RANK

The social life of the Roman world was not entirely separable from its political life, and both were organised for the most part by a strict protocol. As has been seen, members of the senatorial order had the greatest privileges. After them came the equestrian order (*equites* = knights), for which the minimum capital required was 400,000 sesterces. In the theatre both these orders had seating privileges: the orchestra was reserved for senators, and the Roscian Law of 67 BC extended such privilege to the *equites* by allotting them the first fourteen rows of seats behind the orchestra. In origin the *equites* had been cavalry, and up to the second century BC a senator could serve as a knight. But thereafter the cavalry was mainly drawn from auxiliary forces. By that time the interests of the *equites* centred rather on commercial activities like banking and contracting for collection of taxes. They acquired a semi-political power, probably in 123 BC, when control of the juries passed to them from the Senate; this was returned to the Senate under Sulla about 80 BC, but a compromise was reached in 70 giving *equites* a one-third share with senators and *tribuni aerarii* (minimum capital 300,000 sesterces). Augustus was the first to reserve certain important offices for *equites*, notably the governorship of Egypt, which if entrusted to a senator might have produced a dangerous rival. They retained their high position during the Empire, being particularly influential in the third century AD. Every four years under the Republic and every year under the Empire there was a mounted parade and review of the equestrian order.

In addition to having the status of either a senator or an *eques*, a wealthy Roman was likely to command authority both as a head of family (*paterfamilias*) and a patron. The family was a division of the *gens*, and heads of families within a *gens* met for specific business. The legal power of a head of family over its members was at first unlimited, and right through later times he retained very great control. The system of patrons and clients was far-reaching during the late Republic and Empire; and by extension of meaning the word *cliens* came to be used of rulers who formed an alliance with Rome. The patron was a wealthy man who could provide in cash or in kind for his dependants, and if capable would help them in legal matters: the term *patronus* also means 'defending counsel'. The clients were either free citizens or freedmen, in the latter case mostly ex-slaves whose master had become their patron. The system involved the morning greeting, the handing out of a food or monetary dole, and the practice by which some clients often escorted an important man as he made his way down from his house to the political, legal and business areas of central Rome.

## LAW

Roman law was in origin controlled by the *pontifices*, and thus we find religious terminology in early legislation. In 451–450 BC the Twelve Tables were published, laying down prohibitions and specifying the penalties for them. The procedure in civil law, where private individuals were suing and being sued, was unusual. First there was a preliminary hearing, at which a praetor established what the dispute was and appointed a judge (*iudex*), agreed by both sides, to decide it. Since this judge was not necessarily a legal expert, a body of such experts grew up to advise the judges. These were for long mostly nobles, and they had great influence on the collection of a body of legal opinion based on precedent. In the third century AD Ulpian (d 233) and other legal writers summed up clearly the decisions of their predecessors, and in the sixth century Justinian provided for the codification of all legal precedents from Hadrian's time onwards which were still valid. The resulting code has had an important influence on the legal framework of many countries right up to the present.

In criminal law, crimes against the person were tried by a praetor or other magistrate with advisers, while crimes against the State were tried before a public assembly. But there was also provision for a commission of enquiry (*quaestio*) on serious or complicated issues. Out of this last procedure developed a system of permanent *quaestiones* dealing with different types of offence. The first was extortion, then followed poisoning, treason, bribery, violence etc. Since there was no State prosecutor, where as in Verres' trial for embezzlement as governor of Sicily two men claimed to be prosecutor of the same person, one had to be eliminated by a preliminary hearing. In the first century AD trials for treason (*maiestas*) abounded, because a successful prosecutor was rewarded with a quarter of a condemned man's property. *Maiestatem minuere* or *laedere* was the commission of a crime deemed to impair the greatness of the Roman people.

Three points about Roman law show discrimination which would be challenged today. One is that women and aliens had few legal rights and slaves none. Women could not plead in court; the amounts they could legally inherit were limited; and a woman could not, for example, leave money to her children if they were under her husband's *patria potestas* (p 79). The second is the frequency of legal fictions. If, for example, it was thought desirable that a corporation or a foreigner should be party to a case strictly limited to citizens, then by a fiction they could be deemed to be citizens for that purpose. The third is that there was no such thing as a sentence of a term of imprisonment: prisons were for debtors, until their debt was discharged, or recalcitrants, or for persons awaiting trial or execution.

### TAXES

Taxation varied so much from century to century that an adequate summary is not possible. Corresponding to direct taxation were *tributum* and some types of *vectigal*, while other *vectigalia* correspond to indirect taxation. The peoples of Italy were liable to *vectigalia*, though *tributum* was paid by citizens alone as a wealth tax to finance wars up to 167 BC, sometimes on a basis of ultimate return like the post-war credit. Rent on public land was paid to the state, which also gained revenue from mines and salt. Harbour dues were levied at most ports. There was a 5 per cent tax on the value of freed slaves. Augustus introduced a tax on auction sales, a 5 per cent death duty on legacies to non-relatives, and a 4 per cent tax on sales of slaves. *Tributum* was applied in the provinces, under the Republic as a tithe on produce or an individual tax, under the Empire the latter only. Most taxes were collected under the Republic by *publicani*, who were wealthy *equites* with freedmen and slaves working for them, under the Empire by quaestors and imperial procurators.

## CITIZENS

Roman citizenship was acquired by birth, by domicile or by a decree of the people or the emperor. For acquisition by birth either both parents had to be citizens or one a citizen and one a foreigner whose community had an alliance agreement with Rome. Acquisition by domicile came with extension of boundaries or change of status. After the Social War of 91–87 BC all men in Italy south of the Po valley became Roman citizens. Julius Caesar incorporated Cisalpine Gaul, and citizenship came to be extended to free men in recognised *coloniae* and

---

Farmer going to market. Relief of Augustan period, Munich. He is taking a cow and carrying in his right hand a basket of produce, in his left a stick on the end of which is a trussed animal.

Triclinium (pp 88–91) of a house at Pompeii. Three dining-couches surround the small serving-table. Each couch could normally accommodate three diners reclining; the place of honour was the right-hand one on the middle couch.

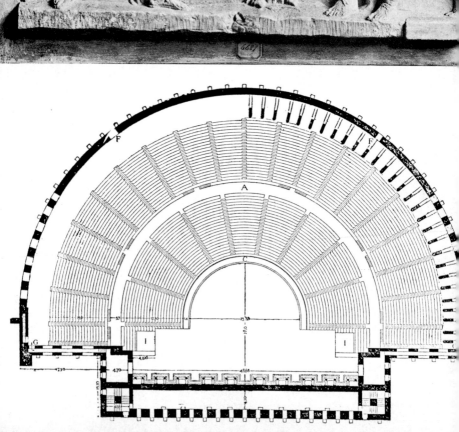

*municipia* in the provinces. During the Empire there was a
tendency for the more important men in the provinces to take
on imperial administrative appointments and thus acquire
Roman citizenship; the Emperor Claudius even allowed certain
Gallic chieftains to stand for Roman magistracies. Soldiers
recruited from the provinces into the auxiliary forces acquired
citizenship when they were honourably discharged, so that the
numbers of citizens were constantly growing. Finally in AD 212,
while the status of local communities was not changed, all free
men in the Empire became Roman citizens. Romans were proud
of their citizenship, and the phrase *civis Romanus sum*, 'I am a
Roman citizen', nearly always conferred dignity and status.

## FREEDMEN

Freedmen and freedwomen (*liberti* and *libertae*) constituted
by the first century BC an important sector of the population.
Horace was happy to proclaim himself the son of a freedman,
and his status did not prevent him from being made a military
tribune by Brutus in time of emergency. The large slave popula-

---

Comic actors. Bas relief, Naples. Sir Arthur Pickard-Cambridge,
*The Dramatic Festivals of Athens*, p 201 (1st ed, Oxford, 1953),
interpreted the scene thus: 'A young man, supported by a slave
and accompanied by a flute-player, is returning intoxicated from
a feast, and is encountered by his father and an elderly friend,
who is trying to calm the paternal indignation.' Only the central
part of the stage is seen (see next figure for typical dimensions).
The purpose of the curtain seems to have been to shut off a door
not used in the play.

Restored ground-plan of the theatre at Aspendus, southern Asia
Minor, second century AD. For details of theatre buildings see
pp 145–6. Below the seats is a channel (C); between the upper
and lower seats a passage (A); on each side were boxes (I).
Diameter of auditorium 95m (313ft); height of stage-buildings
23m (75ft), length 62m (205ft); length of stage 48m 68 (148ft).

tion and the frequency of manumission, whether at an owner's
death or before, resulted in a huge number of freedmen and
freedwomen, especially in Rome. Clever freedmen bilingual
in Greek and Latin were often able to carve out a prosperous
career for themselves. The caricature which Petronius gives us of
the nouveau riche Trimalchio, totally lacking in culture and
taste, is obviously exaggerated but contains many elements of
truth. The most important freedmen were those who were given
special posts by the emperors, eg Augustus' freedman the
learned C. Iulius Hyginus, appointed librarian of the Palatine
libraries, or Licinus, a prisoner from a Gallic or German tribe
who seems to have become procurator of Gaul. The emperor
Claudius extended this system by appointing freedmen virtually
as permanent ministers of state, such as Pallas, who amassed
a gigantic fortune. Although some of these were dismissed
when a new emperor succeeded or a favourite fell, we know of
at least one case where a freedman held on to important posts
of this kind under six emperors. This was the father of Claudius
Etruscus, born in Smyrna about AD 1. He came to Rome as a
slave of the imperial household, started his career as a freedman
of Tiberius, and finished it as late as about AD 90. In Italian
and provincial cities a successful freedman would often be
appointed *sevir*, literally one of a committee of six, or *sevir
Augustalis*, to keep up the religious cult of the emperor. Although freedmen were subjected to certain legal and political
restrictions, their sons were not.

## SLAVES

Slaves were brought to Rome from many different areas,
mostly within the Roman Empire. The majority of them seem
to have come in ships run by slave-dealers. For slaves from Asia
Minor and adjacent areas the market on the island of Delos
provided a convenient intermediate stop. On arrival in Rome
their feet were chalked white, to show that they were for sale,
and they were sold in the slave market. The highest prices

were paid for beautiful boy slaves, as much as 100,000 or 200,000 sesterces, and slave-boys well educated in Greek and Latin fetched fairly high prices. On the other hand an ordinary slave could be bought for as little as 2,000 sesterces (600 is quoted as high for a girl of doubtful character), until in the later Empire they began to be scarce. Slaves had no legal rights, and although writers regularly speak of slaves' marriages these were not legally recognised. Their children born while they were slaves became the property of their master. They were not allowed to own property apart from pocket money; but this exception was often very liberally interpreted. In a law-court the evidence of slaves was not acceptable unless extracted under torture. To our minds this practice seems likely, more often than not, to have produced the opposite result to that intended. If a master was murdered by a slave, all his slaves could be crucified.

The conditions of slaves varied enormously. The most noticeable difference was between the living conditions and treatment of town and country slaves. The town slave had plenty of attractions all round. Although the comedies of Plautus and Terence were adapted from Greek New Comedy, the wine-drinking, cheeky, resourceful type of town slave who was so much a part of these plays must have had many counterparts in Rome. Country slaves, on the other hand, had to work hard on farms or in mills, and gangs of them on *latifundia* (very large estates) were even chained. Slaves who were gladiators had a short expectation of life. So it is not surprising that in 134–132 and 105–101 BC there were slave uprisings in Sicily, a disaffected province. Unrest spread to the mainland and culminated in Spartacus' revolt of 73–71 BC. He and his band of fellow-gladiators broke out of a gladiatorial school at Capua and first occupied Mt Vesuvius, then defeated several Roman armies sent against them, before eventually being rounded up. When this outbreak had been repressed there were no more revolts, but escapes were common. A proposal in the Senate that slaves should wear distinctive clothing was defeated on the ground that they should not be allowed to see how numerous they were. Slaves were used for public works, including road-making, building, mining, construction and maintenance of aqueducts (700 employed on Rome's in the late first century AD), and litter-carrying; and in business concerns such as small pottery and textile industries employing up to 100, and copying of texts.

There was never any crusade against slavery, but thinking Romans tended to treat their own slaves well and deplore ill-treatment of slaves by others. Childless couples quite often freed and adopted their favourite slave. By the fourth century AD the number of slaves was smaller, many households having only one or two, but even two centuries later there was no sign of slavery disappearing. Christianity gave slaves hope and perhaps made some masters more considerate, but priests did not advocate or work for the abolition of slavery.

### RELIGIONS

Religious observance was considered essential to the running of the State, but as territories expanded local cults were incorporated. Roman religion, thought of as something of an obligation or contract, was similar to that of other Italic tribes and parallel in many features to Greek religion; but it also inherited much from the more sombre religion of Etruria. The similarities with Greek cults made it easier to incorporate equivalents to Roman gods and goddesses. Jupiter (*Iuppiter*), the sky-god and ruler of the gods, is the same word in origin as the Greek Zeus, but with *pater* added, and has similar functions. *Zeus*, genitive *Dios*, and *Iup*(*piter*), genitive *Iovis*, both represent an Indo-European *diow* or similar. Venus, on the other hand, seems to be the personification of a noun meaning 'charm', and to have been particularly associated in origin with gardens. But as she was the nearest equivalent to Aphrodite, Greek Goddess of love, she was given Aphrodite's functions as well as her own. In fact the tendency towards personification of abstracts was common, so that among the goddesses worshipped were Fortuna, Concordia, Flora and Roma (the goddess Rome), while the early god Semo Sancus seems to be the holy one of sowing (*semen* = seed, *sancio* = I sanctify). The many taboos indicate primitive origins; indeed the very word *religio* was thought by some to mean 'binding back', ie taboo. Thus the *flamen Dialis*, priest of Jupiter, was forbidden to leave Rome (Augustus allowed a two-night absence), to sleep away from home for more than two nights at a time, to touch a horse or flour or leaven or a dead body, to touch or name a dog, a she-goat, ivy, beans or raw meat, to look at an army, to swear an oath, to wear an ornamental ring, to take off his clothes out of doors, to go out without his headdress, to have a knot in his clothing, to walk under a vine trellis, or to enter a tomb. The college of the pontiffs included *pontifices* themselves, fifteen *flamines*, Vestal Virgins (six in historical times), and a *rex sacrorum* (literally 'king of sacred rites'). The number of pontiffs grew from three to sixteen, and their head was the *pontifex maximus*. Their main function was to advise the presiding magistrate on religious matters, so that the *pontifex maximus* acquired some political power. Augurs, whose numbers grew like those of the pontiffs, had a college of their own; their function was to observe by signs, mostly from birds, whether the gods favoured an action. Another form of divination was practised by *haruspices* (soothsayers), who interpreted entrails, prodigies, and meteorological phenomena. Many Romans were sceptical about soothsayers, and the elder Cato said he was surprised that one soothsayer did not giggle and give the game away when he met another.

Every large city had very many temples; some of those in Rome were of great antiquity. The temple of Vesta, goddess of the hearth, whose flame was kept alight by Vestal Virgins, was circular with a conical roof. In Ovid's time the roof was of bronze, but earlier it was thatched, like the primitive circular huts on the Palatine. Augustus built or restored some ninety-five temples in Rome at a total cost of 100,000,000 sesterces. He boasted: 'I found Rome built of brick and left it built of marble.' The element of propaganda came into it, since emperors could couple a dedication to Rome with one to themselves or their family. Subsequent emperors added to the number of temples, so that a reconstruction of Rome in the age of Constantine makes its centre seem positively cluttered with them. One reason for this was that the Roman system absorbed cults of conquered and even other peoples, apart from Judaism and Christianity which would have nothing to do with polytheism. So there were temples not only of Roman and Italic deities but of imported cults which superstitious Romans were afraid to neglect, eg Magna Mater (Cybele the mother goddess), introduced from Asia Minor in 205–204 BC; Isis, the Egyptian goddess of many names, associated with mysteries; and Mithras, the Persian god of light, especially popular among soldiers. Christianity—along with strictly monotheistic Judaism, of which it was regarded as a sect—was treated differently from other foreign religions, mainly because of the refusal of its adherents to recognise any validity in the traditional Roman religion or to pay any religious homage to the emperor. This challenge to the State was the most serious so far and repression seemed to be called for: Christians, but not Jews, were persecuted. The first persecution came under Nero, who was able by punishing the Christians to divert some of the ill-will caused by the Great Fire of Rome (AD 64). Christianity had first expanded on a large scale in Asia Minor, and it was there that Christians were most persecuted under Domitian. In AD 112 the younger Pliny, appointed special commissioner in Bithynia-Pontus, wrote to Trajan asking whether he had been right in putting to death self-confessed Christians who had been denounced to him. The emperor replied that he had, but that none should be hunted out, that any who recanted should not be punished, and that anonymous accusations should be disregarded. In spite of these measures, by AD 200 Christianity was becoming a dominant force in the Roman Empire. In 303 Diocletian ordered the destruction of churches, but by 325, through Constantine's influence, Roman policy on religion changed completely: the Christian faith came to be recognised as the official religion of the Roman Empire. Pagan religions automatically had to go, though some of their features were incorporated into Christianity; thus the cult of the mother goddess influenced certain Christian approaches towards the worship of the Virgin Mary.

## ASSOCIATIONS

Clubs and guilds started as religious groups, and from about 200 BC had a controlling influence on Roman life. In the first century BC some of these *collegia* and *sodalicia* were used for political purposes. Augustus ruled that all clubs must be approved by himself or the Senate. The scope of clubs and guilds comprised religion (including burial clubs), artisan unions, sport, veterans' associations, local interests etc. Burial clubs, which resembled those started by the poor in the first industrial era of Britain, were allowed to meet not more than once a month. A typical inscription relating to such a one reads: 'It was unanimously resolved that anyone wishing to enter this society shall pay an entrance fee of 100 sesterces and an amphora of good wine, also a five-*as* subscription each month. It was also resolved that anyone who has not contributed for six consecutive months and who dies shall not be given a funeral by the club even if he has made a will mentioning a club funeral.'

## THE CALENDAR

An understanding of the yearly pattern of seasons and of the daily rhythm is essential to any developed society. Complete organisation of a calendar is the mark of a very sophisticated civilisation. The Roman calendar originally comprised ten months, probably with the addition of a winter period not divided into months. This period was subsequently labelled as January and February, but the year started as before in March, which is why September to December literally means the seventh to tenth months. From 153 BC January became the first month. During the Republic there were seven months of only twenty-nine days, so that the total was 355 days; an intercalary month, of twenty-two or twenty-three days, was therefore added when necessary. This tended to be done haphazardly, and Julius Caesar as *pontifex maximus* in 46 BC reformed the calendar, making that year 446 days long to adjust the reckoning, then changed to the present length of year, with a day inserted after 23 February every fourth year.

The three measuring points in each month were Kalends, first day; Nones, fifth, but seventh in March, May, July and October, the longest months by the unreformed calendar; Ides, thirteenth, but fifteenth in the above months. There was no Greek equivalent, so that 'on the Greek kalends' means 'never'. Weeks, although they had been favoured by Hellenistic astrologers, were not a classical system of reckoning, but came in, at first unofficially, in the third century AD. The dates were reckoned before, not after these points, and with inclusive reckoning; a.d. = *ante diem*, the *n*th day before; prid. = *pridie*, the day before. Thus:

Dec 27 = a.d. vi Kal. Ian.

28 = a.d. v Kal. Ian.

29 = a.d. iv Kal. Ian.

30 = a.d. iii Kal. Ian.

31 = prid. Kal. Ian.

Jan 1 = Kal. Ian.

2 = a.d. iv Non. Ian.

3 = a.d. iii Non. Ian.

4 = prid. Non. Ian.

5 = Non. Ian.

The year was reckoned by the names of the two consuls (when Caesar ignored his fellow-consul Bibulus, humorists spoke of the 'consulship of Julius and Caesar'), or, if it was not a recent one, by the number of years since the foundation of Rome, arbitrarily fixed at 753 BC. Thus 1 BC is the 753rd year AUC (*ab urbe condita* = from the foundation of the City), AD 1 the 754th. Christian historians also used, for early dates, the birth of Abraham or the fall of Troy, estimated as 2016 and 1183 BC respectively. From AD 287 levies in kind were subject to annual assessments known as indictions, at first in five-year plans, then from 312 in fifteen-year plans; the years of the indictions came to act as a dating system. The modern practice of calculating years Anno Domini was started by the monk Dionysius Exiguus, who died about 540; he seems to have fixed the birth of Christ a few years too late. The AD system became popular in the Middle Ages, the BC system only comparatively recently.

# 4

# *The Transport Network*

It is obviously not true that all roads led to Rome; nevertheless, Rome became the centre of a road system so highly developed that outside observers could be pardoned for thinking so. There was a 'golden milestone' in Rome, set up in 20 BC, which served as the point of origin for measurement of the many roads leading to the city.

## TRAFFIC CONGESTION IN ROME

Figure 5 shows the public buildings and roads of Rome. The density and type of traffic can be related in part to the different quarters of the city. The Capitoline was a centre of government and worship, the Palatine hill was covered with imperial palaces, the Mons Caelius had temples and other large buildings. The Aventine had changed from a purely working-class area to a business centre where wealthy business-men also lived. The higher parts of the Esquiline, Viminal and Quirinal hills were good residential areas, but many lower slopes were probably occupied by closely packed, overcrowded tenements, the most notorious being the Subura on the down-town side of the Viminal.

Market-places proliferated on the lowest ground between the hills as emperors created new ones named after themselves. The 'forum' marked on the map indicates the dominant market zone of the later period, especially Trajan's. Rome's inner harbour is shown by the *emporium*, a dock warehouse, and the *horrea*, granaries. Large-draught ships could not go above Ostia or Portus.

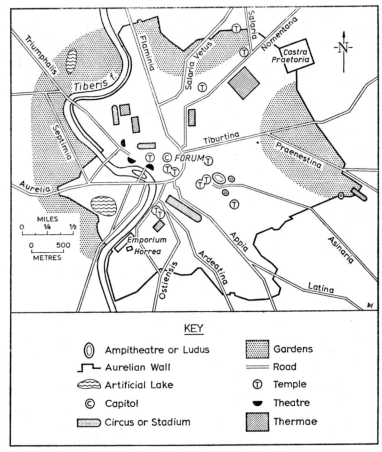

Fig 5   Roads and public buildings in Rome during the Empire

Certainly congestion in Rome was a real problem, at least from the first century BC onwards. From contemporary accounts in Horace, Juvenal (writing about AD 100) and others, we can see that traffic jams, noise and dirt from wheeled traffic, building contractors, animals, etc were just as much of a problem as today. But stronger measures were taken: regulations were introduced controlling the hours during which various types of wheeled traffic were permitted. The following regulation dates from Caesar's time, 45 BC:

*In all streets which are or come to be within the built-up area of Rome, it is forbidden from 1 January next to lead or drive a cart between sunrise and the tenth hour, except for bringing materials necessary for building temples to the gods or public works, or for removing rubble, caused by public demolition, from Rome or from areas of demolition.*

*Carts used for transporting Vestal Virgins, the 'king' in charge of sacrifices and the* flamines *(fifteen priests in Rome), carts used for triumphal processions or for public games held in Rome or within 1 mile of Rome shall be exempted from this law.*

*Carts brought into Rome by night may be moved during daylight hours empty or containing dung for removal.*

## ROADS FOR MILITARY CONTROL

Earlier powers had developed adequate roads, but these tended to be well made only in limited areas, whereas great stretches of Roman roads came to be paved. Besides which, enormously more was accomplished in bridging, embanking and rock-cutting than by other nations. Expansion of roads in Italy was linked with the fact that Rome was basically a land power, turning to the sea where necessary but always having a preference for land communications. In many areas Roman roads have continued throughout the centuries and are the guide-lines of modern communication systems.

The earliest and most famous Roman road was the Via Appia, named after Appius Claudius Caecus, censor, in 312 BC. The road led south from Rome, originally to Capua (S. Maria Capua Vetere) via Tarracina, being extended to Brundisium (Brindisi) in 264 BC or not long after. The period was one of southward expansion, when Rome had defeated the Volsci and was consolidating her gains. The course of the road, known today as Via Appia Antica, can be walked or driven over for 16km (10 miles) from its start in Rome. Whether it was paved during the Republic is uncertain; the earliest paving that we hear of on any roads is in 174 BC. The polygonal stonework of the Via Appia laid down by Hadrian (emperor AD 117–

138) can be seen where the modern tarmac has worn off.

Further expansion took place when the Via Flaminia was built by C. Flaminius in 220 BC, leading up the Tiber and through Umbria to Ariminum (Rimini). The Via Aemilia, built in 187 BC by M. Aemilius Lepidus, ran 280km (175 miles) from Ariminum to Placentia (Piacenza), in long straight stretches with only occasional slight changes of direction. Livy stresses its military importance, as it cut through the territory of the Gallic tribe Boii; but it later had great value as a commercial road, the artery between the agricultural holdings of the Po valley and central Italy.

### SURFACE AND ALIGNMENT OF ROADS

Roads continued to be built throughout most of the period of Roman domination, though after the second century AD far more repair than new work was undertaken. It is most unfortunate that we do not possess any Roman manual of road-making. Only the poet's version has been preserved, and that too in the case of a single road. This is Statius' poem on the Via Domitiana, built by the emperor Domitian in AD 95 to link Sinuessa with Puteoli (Pozzuoli), an important harbour town, and thus make the journey from Rome to the Gulf of Naples much shorter. Statius' description of the actual process of road-making is as follows (*Silvae* iv, 3, 40–55):

*Here the first task was to start the trenches and cut out the balks and excavate the earth thoroughly, throwing it up from deep down. The next task was to replace with a new fill the ditches that had been emptied and to prepare a lower layer for the cambered upper surface, so that the soil does not subside, and that a treacherous foundation does not provide a doubtful resting place for the stones pressed in. Then men have to bind the road by edging-slabs squeezed in on both sides and frequent projecting blocks (gomphi). O what vast gangs are working together! Some are cutting down woods and stripping mountains, some are smoothing rocks and planing timber; others are binding stones and bonding the work together*

*with powdered limestone and black tufa. Others dry thirsty pools
by hand and drive minor rivers far away.*

A good recent interpretation has been made by R. Chevallier,
*Les voies romaines* (Paris, 1971). The first process, marking out
the course, is the same as the first process of modern motorways;
and as with motorways, the construction was done in sections,
in some places of 1 mile each, which could explain the slight
changes of alignment sometimes visible. Because the aim was
directness, one can see in parts of Britain that the lines taken
by motorways correspond to a surprising degree with those
taken by Roman roads. The foundations referred to in the
poem were made of stone, pebbles and sand arranged in
successive layers, and the upper surface was given a camber
to facilitate drainage. Where the road was paved, vertical
slabs were laid at the sides to prevent displacement. The term
*gomphi* may refer to wedge-shaped blocks by the sides of the
road, protruding above the road level, such as have been found
in France and North Africa. In addition to keeping the edges
from damage, they may have served for mounting horses and
for guiding travellers at night.

In the flat Po valley the road system was linked to the allocation of lands to Roman settlers in the early years of the second
century BC. The orientation of the Via Aemilia has strongly
influenced the lines of survey in centuriation squares, mostly
of 20 × 20 *actus*, ie 2,400 Roman feet square or between 705m
(771yd) and 711m (777yd) square. At Caesena (Cesena),
where the hills abut on the plain, the road followed a curved
line along contours; the adjective *curva* is actually used of
the town. At the River Enza, between Reggio Emilia and
Parma, the road deflected from its course to cross the river
at a suitable point, then resumed its original line. The same
love of straight stretches of road may be seen in many parts of
Britain and France, whereas in Italy, apart from the Po valley,
much less straightness in layout is the general rule. A difficult
stretch of the Via Praenestina, which ran from Rome to
Praeneste (Palestrina), has a well-preserved section, paved

with hexagonal slabs; here quite a sharp turn is taken immediately before the road crosses a small stone bridge, which is also well preserved. This is an example of construction for the improvement of gradients on a much used road in undulating land, where straightness had thus to be sacrificed.

### EMBANKMENTS, TUNNELS AND BRIDGES

Embankments were built either to raise roads above marshy ground or to improve the gradient, in that case often coupled with cuttings. Where there was rock, this too could be cut away, as in the Statius passage, and as at Tarracina where for a long time the Via Appia turned inland at right angles to avoid a rocky headland. Later, probably under Trajan, the rock of this headland was cut vertically to a height of 120 Roman feet, the heights being recorded on the rock at intervals of 10ft, to allow for a ledge for the road just above sea level; on that ledge the coastal road has remained to this day. For very hilly sections in less populated areas, as in the Alps or the Pennines, steep gradients were used, where perhaps strategy was more important than frequent commercial travel. No straightness was sacrificed to gradient on the road leading south-east from the Roman fort of Bainbridge, north Yorkshire. It climbs straight out of the valley to a height of 1,900ft (580m), and its inappropriateness for commercial use is borne out by the story of an allegedly unscrupulous contractor in the eighteenth century. Authorised to build a turnpike in the area, he is said merely to have spread a layer of gravel over the disused Roman road; but the turnpike was never used as the gradient was too steep for wheeled transport.

Some steep parts of Roman roads were surfaced with paving, whereas flatter sections might have to manage with a gravel surface: gravel was very commonly used for top dressing in the classical period. The paving was not liable to frost damage, as is the case with modern tarmacadam mountain roads. Tunnels were made but were rare. A famous example was the Crypta Neapolitana, a 550m (600yd) long, narrow tunnel (still existing but closed) at Posilipo north of Naples; since it was not adequately lit, one can sympathise with Seneca's feeling of claustrophobia when he was in it. The Via Flaminia tunnel at the Furlo pass measures 38m 30 (42yd) long, 5m 47 (6yd) wide and 5m 95 (20ft) high, and has an inscription recording that it was made by order of the emperor Vespasian.

Main roads were provided with cylindrical milestones, many of which have survived. Distances are given on these in Roman miles: 5 Roman feet = 1 pace (*passus*, really a double pace), 1,000 paces = 1 Roman mile (*mille passus*, abbreviated MP, c 1·5km (c 1,665yd)). Some roads had longer inscriptions, such as the following from the Via Appia, 6 Roman miles from Forum Appii. 'Sixth milestone. The emperor Trajan, son of the deified Nerva, *pontifex maximus*, in the fourteenth year of his tribunician power [ie AD 110], *imperator* for the sixth time and consul for the fifth, father of his country, had these 19 miles of road paved with flints at his own expense. Rome 49 miles.'

The usual widths were: main roads 20 Roman feet (some stretches were 40 Roman feet wide); subsidiary roads, 12 Roman feet; side roads, 8 Roman feet. A number of streets in Italian towns have preserved more or less their original width, and in fact this and their straightness are often the means of identifying their antiquity.

Temporary bridges were of wood or on pontoons, such as Trajan's pontoon bridge over the Danube. The early permanent bridges were of wood; the wooden *pons sublicius* over the Tiber is associated with a very early period in the history of Rome. Eventually stone became the customary material for important bridges. They were built of strong square blocks, with one arch for small bridges, more for larger ones. The architecture of bridges and of the raised portions of aqueducts is similar, but bridges are wider.

## CANALS

Canals were used for transport mainly to simplify and shorten routes on marshy ground. The Rhône was made navigable for larger vessels by Marius, who in 104–102 BC cut a canal system, the Fossae Marianae, from the river near Grand Passon to the sea near Fos, constructing a new harbour there. For a much grander short cut, Julius Caesar planned to cut a canal across the isthmus of Corinth, to avoid the longer and more dangerous sea journey (a scheme first thought of by the tyrant Periander about 600 BC), but did not live to start operations. A start was made by the emperor Nero with a flourish of trumpets and the cutting of the first sod by the emperor himself; Jewish prisoners were put to work, but the scheme was clearly not completed. Its abandonment was probably due to political reasons rather than to any technological difficulties.

## TRAVELLERS' AIDS

Individual travel by land was not, in time of peace and in civilised parts, a very difficult matter, particularly if one spoke Greek and Latin. One might, according to Juvenal, meet footpads in parts of the Pomptine Marshes or in the Gallinarian pine-forest (south of Paestum), but most areas in Italy were safe enough. The main roads had inns and posting-stations at intervals, where lodging was provided and horses could be groomed or changed. To find their way about, the Romans used either a 'plain' or a 'painted' itinerary. A plain one simply listed the places on each road, with mileages between each, like the itineraries on the sides of early English maps. Of the painted variety our only example is the very fine Peutinger Table, a medieval copy of a road map of the late Roman Empire. This is extremely elongated, being in twelve sections, of which the westernmost, containing nearly all Britain, the whole of Spain, and western Mauretania, is lost. In its extant portion the Table measures 34cm (1ft 1½in) × 6m 74 (23ft). As a result, it looks as if Naples is farther from nearby Pompeii than either is from North Africa! It is clear from ancient maps other than route maps that this type of distortion, resulting in a strip which looks more like a graph than a map, was not the regular practice.

## MEANS OF TRANSPORT

Travel by road was of four types: riding, going by wheeled vehicle, by litter and on foot. The horse was the commonest animal for long-distance riding, but mules were used by those who wanted a cheaper animal. Donkeys were used mainly for going to the fields and for carrying small loads locally; though the man who turned into a donkey in Apuleius' *Golden Ass* certainly seems to have travelled. Wheeled vehicles were of various types: most (the *raeda* was the commonest) were four-wheeled, normally with four horses, while the *cisium* was a light two-wheeled vehicle with two horses. The former were slow (Horace covered only an average of 24 Roman miles a day on his journey to Brundisium), though faster than farm carts. The *cisium* was fast but uncomfortable, with a record of 200 Roman miles in twenty-four hours by changes of horses. There was never anything approaching a public bus service.

The litter (*lectica*), carried usually by four slaves but sometimes by up to eight, was slow but comfortable, and privacy could be ensured by drawing the curtains. It was used most in town, for going to dinner parties and back; but journeys of up to two days were not uncommon. Because of its comfort the litter could serve as an ambulance. The elder Pliny's comment on litters is: 'We walk with the feet of others.' With any of these modes of transport, wealthy people were usually accompanied on journeys by a good retinue of slaves.

## ARMY TRAVEL

Roman army units which used the roads consisted mainly of infantry accompanied by baggage animals. There were also small units of cavalry. The regular day's march was about 20 Roman miles, but much greater distances were covered in forced marches. At 20 Roman miles a day an army would take about fifty-four days to march from Rome to the Channel ports. Letters were for the most part carried by slaves on foot, travelling 20–25 Roman miles a day (50 is the upper limit), or consigned to ships. For the remotest areas this resulted in long delays: Ovid, in exile at Tomis on the Black Sea, laments that for one interchange of a letter each way between a friend in Italy and himself a whole year has elapsed. But it is clear that the great letter-writer, Cicero, had more success, and the tax-farmers (*publicani*) were certainly able to rely on rapid delivery of their correspondence.

On special occasions and for strategic purposes an extra effort had to be made. We are told that, when the army on the Rhine revolted, news of this reached the emperor Galba in about nine days, although he was in Rome 2,100km (1,300 miles) away and the Alps had to be crossed in January. Travel on foot, except for troops and slaves, in order to go any distance was little more popular in ancient than in modern Mediterranean countries, though Galen recommends it from the medical point of view. And the Alps were regarded as horrific, just as they were up to the eighteenth century, certainly not as a tourist attraction; yet Hadrian climbed to the top of Mt Etna, chiefly no doubt from scientific curiosity.

## SEA COMMUNICATIONS

The Romans were less interested in developing sea communications except for heavy merchandise and to serve areas which could not easily be linked by road. From the early days of the Republic, when senators were debarred by a law from owning large ships, they were permitted to own shallow-draught coastal vessels for the transport of produce from their farms. For this type of vessel Rome itself was a port, having great warehouses down the Tiber from the centre, outside the Servian wall beyond the Aventine. Near these may still be seen a vast mound of sherds, the Monte Testaccio, 35m (38yd) high, where successive generations of oil and wine importers dumped broken earthenware. As the urban population increased, Rome came to be dependent for supplies of cheap corn on imports from outside Italy, in particular from Sicily, the North African provinces and Egypt. For these purposes large numbers of merchant ships were constantly coming, even during the winter, to Italian ports. These ships varied considerably in size; some were designed for use both with sail and oars. Some of the largest ships of the grain fleet were as large as 1,200 tons. We even hear of one really outsize ship. The emperor Caligula had this built to transport to Rome from Heliopolis, Egypt, the gigantic obelisk which in ancient and medieval times was in Nero's circus but in 1585 was moved to the square in front of St Peter's. The obelisk weighs 500 tons, and we are told that the ship had a ballast of 800 tons of lentils.

The main harbours to which ships came from the south were Puteoli (Pozzuoli), on the Gulf of Naples, and Ostia, at the mouth of the Tiber. Imports from Greece and Asia Minor, including wine, marble, objets d'art and slaves, also came by sea, especially to Brundisium (Brindisi) and Tarentum (Taranto). Much trade with the Far East likewise relied on sea transport, whereas trade with Spain, which had good road links all the way, without high mountain passes, went mainly by land. Animals for exhibition went both by land and sea, at first from Asia Minor and Africa, later mainly from Africa. Figure 6 illustrates the number and variety of animals, indicating the vast extent of Rome's trading empire. Some are being hunted, and there are also scenes (combined for artistic purposes) of embarkation and disembarkation of animals and birds, including an elephant, a panther and an ostrich.

Passengers preferred to go by land whenever possible. For one thing, the winter weather practically excluded all but the large corn ships and the most sheltered coastal journeys under sail. The regular sailing season was from the first half of March to the first half of November. During this period intending sea travellers would go to a harbour and simply inquire if there was a ship to their destination or nearby, normally being prepared to travel on deck, since the smaller vessels had cabin

Villa of Piazza Armerina
Corridor of the Great Hunt

N

0 1 2 3 4 5m

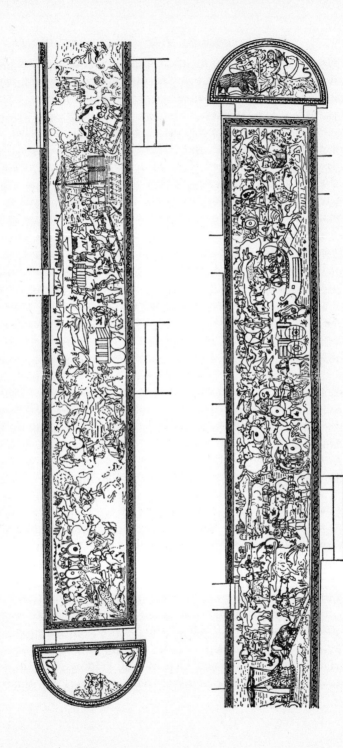

Fig 6 'Corridor of the Great Hunt', mosaic flooring in Sicily from the fourth century AD

accommodation only for the captain and mates. This method of travel might mean a delay in starting, but after that, depending on the winds, speeds of 100–125 Roman miles a day were possible. The greatest numbers of passengers (500–1,000) were carried by the large corn ships mentioned above, plying between Alexandria and Italy. Passengers to Asia Minor preferred not to round Cape Malea, the southern extremity of the Peloponnese, because it was notorious for storms. Instead, they either changed ships at the isthmus of Corinth or their ship was transported over wooden rollers right across the isthmus.

It is interesting to consider whether the Romans had a rule for vehicles and ships to pass each other. In a chariot race the competitors rounded the turning-post (*meta*) anti-clockwise, and this suggests that their rule of the road, where required, was to keep to the right. On the other hand the Portus relief mentioned on p 76 seems to suggest that vessels normally passed each other starboard to starboard, the opposite of modern procedure in confined waters.

Seas outside the Mediterranean were regarded as highly dangerous. A fragment of poetry by Albinovanus Pedo (first century AD) records the horror of those aboard Germanicus' ships when they were swept along on the North Sea in mist with no sight of the coast. On the other hand, merchants were sometimes more daring, even using monsoon winds on voyages to and from India (below) in the age of Augustus.

In the Mediterranean, apart from storms, which can be fearsome especially in winter, there was nearly always the risk of pirates. As early as the fourth century BC we hear that Rome's first naval ventures were due to the need to curb piracy off the west coast of Italy. Most of the later pirates were Greek-speaking and originated in the eastern areas of the Mediterranean. When Julius Caesar was a student he was captured by pirates off Rhodes, vowed to crucify the pirate chief to whom he paid a ransom for his release, and carried out his promise. By 67 BC the pirates had become a serious menace, operating chiefly from Cilicia and Cyprus, and raiding such important trading centres as the island of Delos. A special law was passed in that year empowering Pompey to organise fleets and armies so as to eradicate them, and within six weeks he had divided the Mediterranean into zones, defeated the pirates and settled them on the land. After this the seas became much safer. In the later Empire the Nile delta was a favourite haunt of pirates and brigands; and in general from the third century AD we hear of more frequent kidnappings of travellers and hi-jackings of ships. Nevertheless, there were few periods when it was considered too risky to travel long distances, and there is good evidence that travel for pleasure or for pilgrimage to pagan or Christian shrines was carried out on a very large scale whenever wars did not interfere. This was one of the blessings of the Pax Romana.

### OFFICIAL TRAVEL

As regards travel for official purposes, there was provision for all State employees travelling on business, together with their retinue, to be entertained at the expense of the local community. On the other hand, senators were discouraged from travelling outside Italy by a law forbidding it without valid reason. If they were not on duty, they obtained permission either by acquiring a *libera legatio* (something like a post of ambassador without portfolio) or by claiming that they had to fulfil a vow made to some local shrine. Augustus first organised a system of messengers to relay official mail, then, it seems, changed to one with carriages and relay stations. This served military and civilian needs, and was paid for by local taxation, from which Italy was exempted by the emperor Nerva. Under the later Empire this rapid system of official mail was supplemented by a slower one based on ox-wagons.

Resting-places (*mansiones*) with post-houses were established at regular intervals, averaging about 20 Roman miles, and came under the late Empire to be amalgamated with military posts (*stationes*).

## MAINTENANCE OF ROUTES

Upkeep of roads and bridges was a constant problem. It was supervised by *curatores*, and the work, like that of construction, was carried out by public slaves. Sometimes emperors took on financial responsibility for upkeep of certain sections. There were regulations forbidding encroachment on public roads and compelling landowners to keep certain roads open. A notice on the aqueduct which led 14 Roman miles from the source of the Volturnus to Venafrum read: 'By order of the emperor Augustus, the land for 8ft on each side of the channel made for irrigation has been left free.' There were notices posted up on some private roads, such as the following: 'Private road belonging to Annius Largus. Antonius Astralis is permitted to use it.'

Work was needed at regular intervals to keep harbours open. At Ostia the original harbour, which tended to be silted up by the Tiber, no longer sufficed by the time of the emperor Claudius, who therefore built a new one, Portus, occupying 70ha (175 acres), 3km (1¾ miles) north of Ostia. Then Trajan added an inner basin to provide greater protection against storms. The main naval harbours, at Misenum on the north of the Gulf of Naples and at Ravenna, were essential to the maintenance of the fleet, and work on them was constant. There is evidence that some harbours were abandoned in Roman times as the sea receded. Thus, the decline of Cosa in Etruria between the second century BC and the first century AD was probably connected with the silting up of its port.

## EXPLORATION

Exploration in Roman days resulted in the main from search for minerals, from trade or from military expansion, sometimes building on the discoveries of bold Greek explorers. In the second century BC Eudoxus of Cyzicus, accompanied by a shipwrecked Indian, made a sea voyage from Egypt to India.

He returned laden with spices and other produce, and made a second voyage to India, from which he returned via the West African coast. Another Greek, Hippalus, is credited with the full exploitation of the monsoons to aid voyages to India. It was perhaps his explorations that led Augustus to institute a regular sea service there and back, with 120 ships a year. The elder Pliny (vi. 84 ff) writes that a freedman of Annius Plocamus, a tax-farmer in the principate of Claudius, sailed through the Red Sea and round Arabia to collect taxes, and was then carried by gales to Taprobane (Ceylon): Roman ships with their square sails were not very good at tacking, even if a relief of the third century AD illustrates navigational skill in avoiding collision near the Portus lighthouse. The man spent about six months in Ceylon, learnt the language and made friends with the king, who was so impressed by the uniformity of Roman coinage issued by various emperors that he sent an embassy to Rome. The ambassadors remarked among other things on Roman institutions which did not exist in Ceylon, including personal slavery, tall buildings, late rising and siestas, fluctuating corn prices, and litigation. The fact that Roman exports have been found as far as Korea does not show that any Romans ever reached there, merely that the objects were passed on, perhaps by several intermediaries. Among many explorations for military ends we may mention two. One is that recorded round the north of Britain in AD 84 by Agricola, who established that Britain was an island by sailing round it. Tacitus says that the fleet even sighted Thule, called 'furthest Thule' by other writers, by which he probably meant Shetland. The other was an expedition up the Nile. In 22 BC C. Petronius was sent to repel the Ethiopians of Meroe under Queen Candace. The Romans, like the Greeks before them and many later explorers right into the nineteenth century, were interested in the problem of the source of the Nile. But Petronius, after accomplishing his mission, decided, according to Strabo, that the regions beyond would be difficult to traverse. Augustus made a generous treaty with the queen, while Seneca and other writers were left to speculate on what lay beyond.

## UNITY OF THE ROMAN WORLD

It follows from what has been said that the transport network played a vital part in the concept of unity of the Roman world. From the military point of view, legions and auxiliary forces were able to be moved comparatively rapidly from one province to another. Members of auxiliary forces were usually required to serve in a different province from their own, so that much travel was involved in the process. While Romans were frequently visiting other parts of Italy and somewhat less frequently the provinces, Rome itself, especially from the late first century BC, became full of foreigners of every description: as Juvenal, referring satirically to the main river of Syria, put it, 'the Orontes has long been flowing into the Tiber.' He himself was very familiar with Upper Egypt, but since we can see clearly from his writings that he disliked all foreigners and the Egyptians more than any, and since he seems to have become impoverished, there is quite a possibility that he was exiled there (with loss of property) rather than went voluntarily. Greeks, especially professional men, were constantly visiting Rome; if they were philosophers or astrologers, they ran the risk of expulsion. Romans went to Greece by sea for tourism, education, or even in Cicero's case a mild form of exile, which he spent in Macedonia. So many Spaniards became famous men of letters in Rome that it became a second home to those who felt their cultural interests needed a wider circle. Roman citizenship was constantly extended: by the principate of Caracalla it covered all free men in the Roman Empire (AD 212). With this extension of citizenship and ease of travel, Rutilius Namatianus, writing in AD 416–7, was able, despite the sack of Rome not long before, to address Rome with pride and say to her: 'What used to be the world, you have made into a city.'

# 5

## How They Lived Their Personal Lives

### CLANS AND FAMILIES

IN Roman times the father of a family, *paterfamilias*, occupied a very prominent place, wielding *patria potestas*, 'fatherly power'. He had in the earlier period power of life and death over all members of his *familia*. This term means either 'family' or 'household', since it could include not only all unmarried sons and daughters but all household slaves. For matters of inheritance or common policy, the father would be the family representative at a meeting of all heads of families in the *gens*, each *gens* being essentially a group of families. Membership of the *gens* was passed on to his children, though daughters who married took on the *gens* of their husbands. Adopted children would also be members of their adoptive father's *gens*. The practice of adoption was common, especially in the highest families, sometimes for reasons of inheritance, sometimes for political reasons. As in the clan structure, a name (in this case the middle one) was common to all members of a *gens*.

### NAMES

The first name of a freeborn Roman male was his *praenomen*. The usual *praenomina*, with their abbreviations, were:

| A. Aulus | L. Lucius | Ser. Servius |
| C. Gaius | M. Marcus | Sex. Sextus |
| Cn. Gnaeus | P. Publius | T. Titus |
| D. Decimus | Q. Quintus | Ti. Tiberius |

The abbreviations C. and Cn. were established before the Romans created the letter G and were never displaced by it. Conversely, it is incorrect to write Caius for Gaius.

The second name (*nomen*) designated the *gens*. Thus some of the commonest *nomina* under the Republic, out of a large number, were:

| | | |
| Aelius | Furius | Plautius |
| Aemilius | Horatius | Porcius |
| Aquilius | Iulius | Quinctius |
| Caecilius | Iunius | Sempronius |
| Calpurnius | Licinius | Servilius |
| Cassius | Livius | Sulpicius |
| Claudius | Lutatius | Terentius |
| Cornelius | Manlius | Tullius |
| Domitius | Marcius | Valerius |
| Fabius | Papirius | Verginius |
| Fulvius | | |

Women originally had no legal name, but the practice arose of giving them *nomina*, with ending -*a* for -*us*, followed if necessary for identification by the genitive of their father's or husband's name. This did not avoid duplication of sisters' names, and *maior, minor* or diminutives were often employed.

The third name (*cognomen*) was a differentiating name, either the same as the father's or purposely varied from his. These *cognomina* were drawn from deformities, nicknames, occupations, places of origin (often of the family rather than of the individual), titles of honour etc. Thus Flaccus = flabby, Naso = with the nose, Faber = smith, carpenter, Scipio = staff, Maximus = greatest, Numidicus = conqueror in Numidia. For the name derived from an occupation we may compare, in Wales, 'Dai Jones butcher', 'Dai Jones baker'.

Apart from emperors, to whom special rules apply, a man

was rarely known by his *praenomen* alone except by his close friends. Others would, in addressing him, couple it with either his second or his third name, and often we find a variation between the two in the same man, eg Cicero may be known as Tullius (earlier English 'Tully'). In writing of him they either included or excluded the *praenomen*. An additional name (*agnomen*) might be given to mark a particular characteristic or achievement or, in the case of an adopted son, the original *gens* name, eg Aemilianus was a man who had started life as an Aemilius.

## CARE OF CHILDREN

At birth a child was lifted up by its father to indicate that he had accepted it as legitimate. Young children were dependent on their mothers, who looked after them personally. A large number of inscriptions tell us of great love between mothers and their children, and much of this should be regarded as genuine. The death-rate among children, to which occasional exposure of deformed children or baby girls contributed, was comparatively high. Funerary inscriptions point to the great sense of loss and affection for those who died as young children. Boys and girls in their turn were brought up to observe *pietas* towards their parents. *Pietas* was not normally 'piety' but a sense of duty towards one's parents, the State, the gods, and under the Empire the emperor as 'father of the fatherland'.

On the eighth or ninth day after birth a baby was purified, and was given small presents which were strung together to form a necklace. Children often wore over their tunic a *bulla*, a gold, bronze or leather circular locket with attachment; it was once confined to patricians. Young people of good birth wore, for formal occasions, a purple-bordered toga curiously similar to that of magistrates. When males reached the age of fourteen to seventeen, they laid aside this *toga praetexta* and ceremonially assumed the *toga virilis*, 'toga of manhood'. Younger girls and the children of poor people wore a tunic as their outer garment.

### BIRTHDAYS

Birthdays were celebrated by propitiating the *genius* in the case of a man, the *Juno* in the case of a woman. This was thought to be a divine spirit living in a person, born at his birth and dying at his death. The *genius* would naturally be pleased if the celebrator of the birthday drank plenty of good wine! We find Lucan's widow celebrating his birthday long after his death and Statius writing a poem for this occasion.

### MARRIAGE AND DIVORCE

Engagements were made by arrangement between the fathers or guardians, unless the fiancé was legally independent. A ring or other token was given as an engagement present. Under the Republic and early Empire engagements were informal, but under the late Empire legal contracts were introduced. On the day before the wedding the bride gave up her *toga praetexta* and put on the bridal gown, *tunica recta*, 'straight tunic', so called because it was woven vertically. She also wore a flame-coloured veil, with a garland of flowers under it, and saffron-coloured shoes. Her hair was divided into six ringlets by a spear-shaped curling iron.

On the wedding day, after the auspices had been taken, the marriage contract was signed by the fathers or guardians. The bride did not have a bridesmaid but a *pronuba*, who was a married woman. The *pronuba* brought bride and bridegroom together and saw that they joined hands. Then those taking part prayed to the gods and goddesses associated with weddings, especially Juno, and offered a sacrifice to Jupiter. This was followed by good wishes to the bridal pair and a wedding feast in the house of the bride's parents. Plautus, in the *Aulularia* (Pot of Gold), is able to have fun at the expense of the miser who is duty bound to lay on such a feast but finds all the food for it costs too much; he buys his daughter as a wedding present only a little packet of incense and a small bunch of flowers, while a neighbour comes to the rescue by providing a sheep to cook. In the evening after such a feast came the most ceremonious part of the wedding celebrations. A pretence was made of tearing the bride from her mother's arms, thus harking back to the old days of violence typified by the Rape (= seizing) of the Sabines. The bride was then escorted in a torchlight procession from her father's house to the bridegroom's. Music was provided by flute-players, and the procession was joined by a good number of people, who sang wedding songs and a rough type of banter called Fescennine verses. The bride carried three one-*as* coins, one each for the bridegroom, his household gods, and the gods of the crossroads. On arrival she anointed the doorposts and hung garlands on them, as a form of dedication. She said the words *ubi tu Gaius, ego Gaia*, 'where you are Gaius, I am Gaia'; this was just symbolic of their unity, since neither changed *praenomen*. The bridegroom carried her over the threshold in case she should slip and cause a bad omen. After this he presented her with fire and water, as a token that she was now the mistress of the house (a law forbidding a man fire and water in effect exiled him). Slaves' marriages were not recognised by the law, but in common parlance and current practice they existed everywhere.

Divorce, which has only recently been permitted in modern Italy, was common in ancient Rome, especially among the wealthier families. Caesar divorced his wife Calpurnia after the Bona Dea (good goddess) scandal, in which P. Clodius disguised himself as a woman to penetrate a women's religious gathering (62 BC). 'Caesar's wife', proclaimed her husband, 'must be above suspicion.' Cicero, who had frequent mild quarrels with his wife Terentia, especially over money matters, divorced her after about twenty-three years of married life. Women had few legal rights, and a woman could not divorce a man.

### DEATH

Death scenes are often found on sarcophagi. The body was laid on the ground, and a relative closed the eyes, while those present wept loudly. A poor person's funeral was a simple affair: recorded burial costs average about seven times as much in Italy as in North Africa. In the case of wealthier persons undertakers and their slaves made preparations for the funeral: a procession with torches (originally all funerals were at night) was headed by musicians playing a dirge and hired mourners; at the forum a funeral oration was pronounced. Cremation was the usual custom from the first century BC to the second century AD, though certain families retained the custom of burial, which had been the earlier. Under the Antonines and later, burial again became the commoner; it was invariable for Christians.

Attempts have been made to assess the expectation of life from ages at death recorded on tombstones. The main conclusion is that expectation was lower than in modern Europe, and lower still in North Africa and among the slave population. Certain individuals lived quite as long as today.

———

Butcher's shop. Relief, second century AD (Dresden, originally Rome). The butcher's wife, seated, is entering the accounts on wax tablets. Note the scales behind the assistant.

Soft furnishing and drapery. Relief in Uffizi Gallery, Florence. Two slaves display material to a woman customer. Hanging on the rail above are made-up items.

NAVI NARBONENSES

SIN̅T̅ SABRATENSIVM

## HOMES

Houses differed in town and country and between rich, less prosperous and poor. The younger Pliny had a small house at least seventy-five years old in Rome, but also an estate at Novum Comum (Como) and a palatial villa south of Ostia. Remains of town houses can best be studied at Pompeii and Ostia. Of the two, Pompeii represents a more cultured, leisured and wealthy society, with Oscan and Greek elements, while Ostia, near the mouth of the Tiber, is a harbour town lacking many of the trimmings of Pompeii except for a certain magnificence in its public buildings. Instead of looking out on to the street, many Roman houses, as in parts of the Mediterranean and the Iberian peninsula today, looked inward to a courtyard. It was, in fact, quite common for the ground floor at street level, each side of the main entrance, to be occupied by purpose-built shops, owned either by the houseowners or the shopkeepers. At Ostia, dating from about AD 100, there were also blocks (*insulae*, literally 'islands') of tenements between three and five storeys high. It is clear from literary allusions that similar tenement blocks existed in Rome.

---

Mosaic floor in the Forum of the Corporations, Ostia, third century AD. It was in the office of the corporation of Narbo (Narbonne), capital of southern Gaul. Inscription: NAVI (CVLARI) NARBONENSES, 'shipowners of Narbo'. The ship is being unloaded by a hoist at a warehouse.

Another mosaic floor in the same Forum, belonging to the corporation of Sabratha, Tripolitania. Inscription: STAT(IO) SABRATENSIVM, 'Sabratha office'. The elephant, clearly African, may indicate important trade in ivory from tropical Africa through Sabratha, which acquired the status of a Roman colony in the second century AD.

Figure 7 is a plan of a typical house based on several houses at Pompeii and Herculaneum. A = *alae*, literally 'wings' (p 92); B = bedroom; L = lavatory; S = food store. The main reception room was called the *atrium*, a name originally connected with the dark smoke from the fire. Although the *atrium* was never a very light room, the name was quite inappropriate to its elegance in the later days of underfloor heating. From the second century BC it had in its centre an *impluvium*, a shallow square depression into which rainwater fell from a skylight.

Near the *atrium* was the *triclinium*, dining room. This was so called from the most usual arrangement of furniture, three couches round a square table, the fourth side being left open for serving. Men and women dined together, both reclining on cushions. The normal arrangement of couches in the *triclinium* was for up to three to recline on each couch, with the family couch on the left and the others kept for guests (pp 50–1). With this arrangement the maximum number at table was nine. Cicero sneers at Piso for allegedly occupying the whole of one side while he squeezed five into another. An alternative arrangement, introduced in the late Republic, was a single semicircular couch seating six to eight people.

Roman furniture varied from the utilitarian to the highly ornate. Dining-tables were wooden and normally square, though we hear also of extravagant tables with circular or oval tops formed from a complete section of a tree: Cicero paid 1,000,000 sesterces for a citron wood table. Small ornamental tables were most often of imported marble with circular tops. Chairs and beds were mostly wooden, sometimes with fine ornamentation. The base of the bed could have leather webbing. Couches either had ends but no backs, following a pattern popular in Greece, or had backs like sofas. Under the early Empire sideboards, cupboards and bookcases came into more general domestic use. Rugs rather than carpets were laid on the floors.

Kitchen furniture included tables, stools, tripods and braziers. Among cooking utensils were bowls, pots, ladles, meat-hooks, knives, spoons, sieves etc.

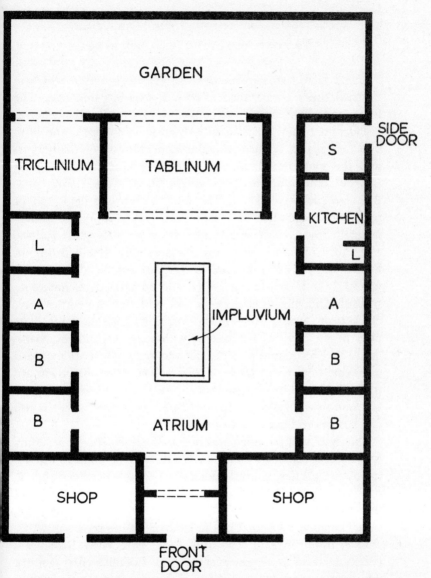

Fig 7   Composite plan of Roman house in Italy. For key see opposite.
There might be an upper floor over the rear quarters

### EATING, SLEEPING AND BATHING

There were two, or sometimes three, meals a day, which in classical times were called *ientaculum*, *prandium* and *cena*. The first was a light breakfast, consisting of bread and cheese or bread and honey (occasionally dried fruit or eggs), and with milk for a drink. We hear of children, people on a diet, labourers and the gluttonous emperor Vitellius taking it, although it was not a regular meal for adults. Bread varied from pure white to coarse plebeian. The lunch comprised eggs, fish or pork, with vegetables or mushrooms, and fruit. Wine, usually watered down, could be drunk with the meal, while *mulsum*, a mixture of honey and wine, was usually drunk before it. Dinner was the great meal of the day, and for the fairly wealthy was likely to be made up of eggs, cold hors d'oeuvres including shellfish and olives, fish, game and pork (or sometimes veal, chicken or lamb), fruit and sweets, with wine as drink. The poor might have to be content with soup, vegetables, coarse bread and occasional pork. About 150 types of fish are recorded as having been eaten by the ancients. The price of fish was apt to reach absurd heights, so that the elder Cato (second century BC) moralised: 'What can one expect of a city where a fish can cost more than an ox or a cow?'

The system of reclining was not practised by slaves, and only to a limited extent by children. We do hear of children attending dinner parties, but it does not seem to have been customary; otherwise they presumably ate in the kitchen. Slaves were kept busy cooking, attending to guests, serving and washing up; they had their own food in the kitchen, sitting on stools.

Over-indulgence in food and drink by wealthy Romans is commented on at almost every period. Lucullus (first century BC), whose name tends to be used by gourmet restaurants on the Continent, was accustomed after the end of his military career to spend 200,000 sesterces on a really elaborate dinner-party. Under the early Empire an official dinner for a large number of guests might cost 1,000,000 sesterces. Peacocks, whole boars, *foie gras*, pigs stuffed with various delicacies, exotic fish— all these were among the items which contributed to such fantastic expenses. Among wines, Falernian was the favourite Italian and the wine of Chios the most expensive Greek. Wine was drunk mixed with water by most people, but ordinary wine was cheap, and slaves in particular were given to excessive drinking (Fig 8).

Fig 8　Wine-cart, from a Pompeii fresco showing two slaves each handling an amphora

The stricter moral code of many Romans brought about legislation against the luxuries of the wealthy over two centuries. There were constant sumptuary laws, with the following provisions:

182 BC　Limit on numbers of guests at dinner parties.
161 BC　Limit on expenditure at dinner parties; prohibition of serving of fatted hens.
143 BC　Provisions extended to the whole of Italy.
115 BC　Prohibition of serving of dormice, shellfish, and birds from outside Italy.
89 BC　Prices of expensive wines fixed.
78 BC　Prices of expensive foods fixed.
? BC　Magistrates forbidden to go to private dinner parties (this was intended as a measure against bribery).

46 BC   Julius Caesar: some foods forbidden; earlier maximum expenditures revised to take account of inflation.

22 BC   Augustus: entertainment maxima, fixed somewhat higher for special feast days.

AD 16   Gold vases for private use and men's silk clothing prohibited.

As the emperor Tiberius realised, there was little point in legislation of this sort, since most of it was too difficult to enforce.

It is not surprising that Galen, the famous Greek doctor who went to Rome in AD 164, wrote: 'Most of our chronic infirmities require a slimming diet. This remedy will often solve the problem without any need for medicine.' His own slimming diet included various kinds of raw vegetable with vinegar; and he advised his readers, among other things, to eat meat or poultry of a suitable kind for their condition, eg sedentary workers should eat wings of poultry or game.

Not only the arrangement of the *atrium* and *triclinium*, but that of the subsidiary rooms differed according to area and status. Many houses had a *tablinum*, often regarded as part of the *atrium*, with windows opening on to a portico and garden. We should perhaps call this a study: the name means archive room, since family documents were kept there.

Passages led from the *atrium* to men's and women's quarters. In the case of a noble family (one which had had male-line ancestors of curule rank, ie consuls, praetors or curule aediles), these passages would have wax masks called *imagines* of such ancestors stored in cupboards in the *alae* (A. Fig 7). When anyone in the family who was of similar rank died, these masks were paraded at his funeral by hired mummers. The word for ancestors, *maiores*, is the plural of the adjective meaning 'greater'; similarly *antiquior* may mean not only 'more ancient' but 'preferable'. Romans of standing were brought up to venerate their ancestors, and the great deeds of heroes of the past were constantly brought forward as *exempla*, examples of good qualities or praiseworthy conduct.

Men's and women's quarters were normally separate except for a room for husband and wife. Younger children seem to have slept in the women's quarters. Only a very few houses have been found with sleeping accommodation clearly designed for slaves, but evidence suggests that attic dormitories were the commonest for them. Other features would be a kitchen with small rooms off, a bathroom, a water-closet, and in the wealthier houses a library. Baths were heated by hypocausts, with brick pillars similar to those in the public baths. These were often extended as a heating system to a few rooms in the house, particularly in the colder northern provinces.

### ART IN THE HOME

Statuary was to be found in private houses and gardens, in forums and in public buildings. It consisted of full-sized or even colossal statues, busts or statuettes. The Romans liked their statues in large numbers, as the Etruscans had before them: Pliny tells us that in 267 BC there were 2,000 bronze statues at Volsinii in Etruria. An element of prestige and propaganda affects its use in private houses and gardens, since it could commemorate famous ancestors; we may compare the *imagines* mentioned above. This resulted in a certain idealisation of facial features. But we also find, as with Hellenistic statuary, some extreme realism, with wrinkles, warts and all.

Paintings in houses were mainly in the form of murals. The frescoes of Pompeii show many mythological subjects, and copies of famous Greek paintings of the fifth and fourth centuries BC were popular. In the latest period at Pompeii (see below) a favourite theme of murals was fantastic architecture and landscaping, with buildings seemingly rising in one tier behind another. In these there is a noticeably different approach to perspective from today's. By comparing the styles of painting with the archaeological evidence, scholars have attempted to establish a sequence of painting styles for Pompeii (shown in the table below) and, with certain adjustments, for other places.

The date given here indicates what was thought to be the approximate starting date at Pompeii; but doubt has been thrown on the scheme, which must be considered less certain as it progresses, and there is some overlap.

| Style | Date | Name | Features |
|---|---|---|---|
| I | 150 BC | Incrustation | Coloured stucco to imitate marble |
| II | 80 BC | Architectural | Mythological and religious themes, with use of perspective |
| III | ? AD 14 | Egyptianising | Framed panels, with styles adapted from the miniature |
| IV | ? AD 62 | Ornamental | Fantastic architecture and long vistas |

Mosaics were constructed out of small pieces of marble, precious stones or tiles. Their commonest use was for ornamenting floors, but they are found also on walls. Mosaic (tessellated) pavements consisted either of geometrical patterns or of pictures, with quite a variety of colouring used. Animals are a common theme: a well-known Pompeii mosaic has a dog with the words *cave canem*, 'beware of the dog'. Some of the animal scenes are taken from fights in the amphitheatre, among the most notable being those found at Piazza Armerina (Sicily), several places in North Africa, and Antioch. Piazza Armerina mosaics discovered in 1917 show girls wearing bikinis. Another well-known theme was the four seasons, which were depicted one on each side or corner of a square mosaic. A less 'bourgeois' artist of Pergamum imitated in mosaic the unswept floor of a dining-room which resulted from guests at a dinner-party throwing down shells, fruit-stones etc. Patrons of literature or philosophy could commission mosaic themes illustrating their interests. Thus at Low Ham, Somerset, there is a series of scenes from the *Aeneid*; on the island of Mitylene were found mosaics with a number of scenes from Menander's comedies; at Cologne there is a mosaic showing the heads of famous philosophers. In the same category as mosaics is what was called *opus sectile*, which was fitted together from much larger thin slabs of coloured marble.

### GARDENS

Gardens were formal, in a style much more closely approximating to the later Italian than to English. They were integrated with colonnades, statuary and pools or fountains, and had paved walks and bowers. Among the flowers and bushes most popularly grown were box hedges, which were the precursors of the formal Italian garden, oleanders, and bay-trees; roses, lilies and violets. For roses the most famous area was Paestum, while Tarentum was well known for its mild climate and horticulture. Virgil writes of an old man from Asia Minor who only had a poor plot near Tarentum (*Georgics* iv. 130–7):

> *Yet here among the thorns*
> *He grew a kitchen garden, and all round*
> *White lilies, vervain and the slender poppy,*
> *Rivalling wealth of kings, and coming home*
> *Late every evening, loaded up his store*
> *With home-grown feasts. He was the first to pluck*
> *The rose in spring, the apple in the autumn,*
> *And when grim winter broke the rocks with cold*
> *And halted flowing water with its ice,*
> *He was already gathering the flowers*
> *Of tender irises.*

### LIFE IN ROME

Life in Rome was originally simple and not very different from life in the countryside. Livy and others were no doubt right in saying that in the fifth century BC Cincinnatus, when called upon to be dictator, was hard at work farming his seven-*iugera* (1·76ha/4·7 acres) estate just the other side of the Tiber. But gradually town and country became very different, with a special routine for the life of the city. There the important man was visited between daybreak and the second hour by his friends and clients; that was known as the *salutatio*, 'greeting'. This custom was closely linked with the patron-client relationship and with the practice of distributing the *sportula*, originally a basket of food but later money in lieu of this. Since legacy-hunting was rife, one could expect those who hoped for legacies to turn up regularly each morning with flattering words for the wealthy, especially childless widows. The practice of *salutatio* was probably not such a farce as Martial and Juvenal portray, but it was certainly a boring and time-consuming one. It had its origins in a system of informal family advice. Horace writes (*Epistles* ii. 1. 103ff):

> *At Rome it was a pleasant custom once*
> *To open up one's house in early morning,*
> *Reveal the law to clients, lend out cash*
> *Secured on good accounts, defer to age*
> *And teach a young man what makes money grow,*
> *Or how wild fancies whittle it away.*

At the third hour the business of law-courts began. Important men spent a fair amount of their mornings in the central area of Rome dealing with either senate business or committees or legal and personal problems. Members of the senate were compelled to live in Rome and attend, theoretically, all its meetings. Morning was also the meeting-time for popular assemblies, either for elections or for legislative business. It was likewise the time for commercial business or political discussion in the Forum; just as in Greek cities, much of this was transacted out of doors. The younger Pliny, no doubt telescoping somewhat, writes (*Epistles* i. 9): 'Today I took part in a *toga virilis* ceremony, attended an engagement or wedding; one man called me in to witness a will, another to support him in the law-courts, another to give him legal advice.' As a substitute for newspapers there was the sheet known as Acta Diurna, 'Transactions of the Day', posted up in the Forum to show briefly what had happened in the last twenty-four hours and what events were scheduled for the day. Women spent the morning giving orders to slaves for buying what was needed, seeing that all was in order in the house, talking to friends and attending to the children. The talk was not always just gossip, since it is clear from Cicero's letters that women had an important background influence on political developments as well as having interests in property. Where there were special hours for women in public baths, they seem to have been in the morning.

The lunch (*prandium* in classical times) was taken about the sixth hour, midday, and after this and perhaps a siesta, the afternoon was spent by many Romans on exercise and going to the baths. A busy lawyer or politician would cut out all or some of this, and work on through the afternoon, while an assiduous writer like the elder Pliny continued reading or writing. Then came dinner, *cena*, which in society circles was a long meal, the only one to which guests were regularly invited. It usually started about the ninth hour in summer, the tenth in winter. We are told that the elder Pliny was thought unusual to spend no more than three hours on it, and may wonder whether these were summer or winter hours, since such a period would vary between approximately $2\frac{1}{4}$ and $3\frac{3}{4}$ modern hours. The dinner party might be attended by parasites, who were expected to lay on some entertainment in return for their dinner, and sometimes music or poetry reading formed part of the entertainment.

The dress worn by senators and many others in Rome was the toga, a voluminous woollen garment which must have been roughly semicircular in shape before being wound round the shoulders and waist. It had no real pockets, only a fold in which possessions could be kept. The toga worn by curule magistrates was *praetexta*, purple-bordered. Men attending the morning *salutatio* were expected to wear a clean toga.

### LIFE IN THE COUNTRY AND PROVINCES

In the country, wealthy Romans who owned villas imported to them some of the habits of the city. For most people, however, life in the country was less leisured and less formal than life in Rome. Work on the farm occupied a large percentage of the daylight hours, and Columella says that in winter there are many jobs that can be done by lamp-light. The mere fact of owning slaves did not mean that the master could take things easily. Free labourers as well as slaves were often employed, and the farmer's calendar shows a respite only for a month from 13 December. In many parts of the country there would be little difference between a public holiday and a working day; though a small town could be expected to have what Juvenal (iii. 173) calls a grassy theatre in which the occasional play was performed on a festival day. As to dress, as Juvenal implies, the toga can almost be thought of as a city dress for Rome alone: it was hardly ever worn in many other parts of Italy. There the plain tunic was the outer garment, and for travelling a cloak was worn over it. Horace is keen to stress that the country dinner which he lays on for guests at his Sabine farm (*Epistles* i. 5. 2) will be simple and vegetarian. But since we know that even earlier he had eight slaves there, he is perhaps indulging in mock-modesty induced by comparison with the more lavish establishments of his city friends. In one of his poems (*Epistles* i. 14) he contrasts himself with his farm bailiff: the bailiff, who lives in the country, is constantly longing for the flesh-pots of Rome ('greasy cookhouse' is one phrase), while Horace, kept in Rome by business, is equally longing for the country.

In the cities of the more civilised provinces there was an attempt to copy life in Rome. Large numbers of Roman citizens lived in the provinces, side by side with the provincials, yet forming in each place a community which could be called on, for example, to advise the governor. It is noteworthy that in many of the cities of Spain such excellent Latin was spoken as to differ hardly at all from the best Latin. The schools of Burdigala (Bordeaux), Tolosa (Toulouse) and other places in Gaul were pre-eminent in the fourth century AD for their studies of Latin language and literature. In the Greek-speaking provinces, ie Achaea, Macedonia, the provinces of Asia Minor, Sicily, and some coastal settlements elsewhere, life went on in much the same way as before the Roman conquest apart from the loss of independence, with Greek as the *lingua franca*. Amenities in the larger cities of the provinces were very complete, with large monumental public buildings, and almost every facility available in Rome was available there too. The great numbers of shops in many provincial cities bear witness to their prosperity under the Empire. They were not related only to size of settlement, since some of the smaller towns were obviously most sophisticated. But in the more barbarian provinces, and in some rural parts of others, life was certainly harder. In many the population was used to a simple local diet, and with greater poverty the range of goods purchasable was much smaller. Ovid, accustomed to the luxurious life of Augustan Rome, was disgusted at the uncivilised life, poor facilities and what he considered appalling climate of Tomis (Tomi) on the Black Sea, to which he was exiled. If, for example, he had been allowed to spend his exile in Athens, he would have found flourishing literary and philosophical circles and the spirit of enquiry which is referred to in the Acts of the Apostles, 17. 21: 'The Athenians in general and the foreigners there had no time for anything but talking or hearing about the latest idea.'

## HEALTH

Sanitation in Roman houses, though not completely perfect, was much better than in later times right up to the nineteenth century. The wealthier houses, both in town and country, had their own baths and water-closets. Where the owner was not regularly in residence, the water was not kept heated. Thus, when the younger Pliny had announced that he would be visiting his villa near Ostia, the slaves heated up the baths. But if he arrived without notice, he normally went to public baths in Ostia, of which there were three establishments. Latrines were when possible connected to a main drainage system. At Rome the main drain, *cloaca maxima*, was very soundly constructed. Even in a provincial garrison town like Eburacum (York), recent excavations have revealed a drain (p 104) serving the lavatories of a fairly large group of houses. Fresh water supply was obtained from aqueducts, of which Rome had ten by the first century AD, increasing to fourteen by the late Empire, and of which many other towns had at least one. The water was collected in square reservoirs and from these piped off in lead pipes to private houses. Since skeletons have shown evidence of lead poisoning, it has been suggested that the prevalence of lead piping was very injurious to the health of Romans. Certainly ancient writers showed themselves familiar with its dangers, and Vitruvius recommended the use of earthenware rather than lead pipes wherever possible.

Medicine and surgery in Rome were mainly in the hands of Greeks, most of whom were freedmen. The Hippocratic writings had reached a very high level by 400 BC, so that as heirs to a sound body of teaching on such items as fractures and dislocations doctors were able to render first-class service. When it came to the introduction of new cures, on the other hand, there were too many quacks. As today, doctors strove to find answers to problems not fully understood, and some of these worked. In 23 BC Augustus seems to have been cured of a mysterious liver disease by his doctor Antonius Musa, who prescribed something very reminiscent of nineteenth-century hydropathic ideas, a cold bath treatment and a lettuce diet. Horace tried the treatment but does not report its effect. It did not work for Augustus' nephew Marcellus, who died shortly afterwards. Many spa establishments, especially those with hot springs, became famous as resorts for the infirm. The good water supply and sanitation obviously protected the Romans from the diseases which attacked crowded cities in the Middle Ages. But one cannot expect great advances with teachers like the Greek under Nero who claimed to be able to train an unskilled slave to become a qualified doctor in six months. The ancients' lack of knowledge of the ways in which germ diseases are spread is evidenced in their inability to cope with malaria. Like other diseases it was put down to a disequilibrium of the four fluids or humours in the body: blood, phlegm, yellow bile and black bile. This mosquito-borne infection is thought to have become prevalent in the marshy areas of Italy and Sicily, especially during the later Empire. If we believe certain scholars, it was a significant factor in the decline and fall of Rome.

Dentistry was a part of medicine. The Romans regarded toothache as one of the greatest torments. They were unable to fill teeth but did extract, and artificial teeth were sometimes carved from ivory. However, dental hygiene was extensively advocated with the use of tooth picks and tooth powder, and bad breath was a subject of ridicule.

# 6

## *How They Worked*

An advanced and highly organised civilisation, Rome and its empire must have had a working force almost as varied as ours. Allowing for the differences in energy, mostly slave-based instead of dependent as ours is on fossil fuels, the proportion of workers engaged on primary, manufacturing and service industries was probably not very different from much of Europe, at least up to the nineteenth century. The list of manufactured consumer goods from any large excavation site indicates workers in most trades comparable with those round any but the most modern cities.

---

Fullers, seen on these frescoes from Pompeii, first century AD, now in Naples, were the forerunners of laundries, dyers and cleaners (p 118). (1) One slave treads down the cloth in a tub of water and soda (the Romans had no soap), while others are rinsing. (2) One young man brushes the cloth; another carries a wickerwork frame over which it will be draped, so that the fumes of the sulphur will cause bleaching. The lady and girl discuss a piece of work. (3) The seated female slave is cleaning a brush. The boy appears to be handing over a garment.

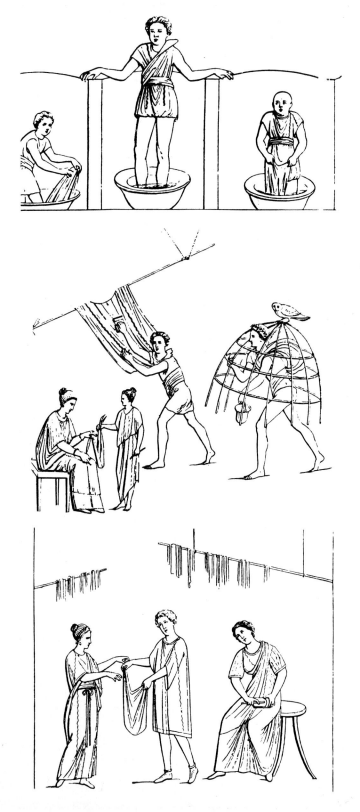

### FARMING AND FISHING

But Rome had its origins in a pastoral and agricultural community, and agriculture continued throughout its history to be one of the prime concerns. Figure 9 shows the outer limit of olive cultivation and the most important crops, as well as the principal minerals (gold, silver, iron, copper, sulphur). From the specialist writers on agriculture, headed by the elder Cato, and from Virgil's poem *The Georgics*, we are well informed about types and methods of farming. The concern of the State with agricultural education is illustrated by the fact that the Senate, probably in or after 146 BC, ordered a Punic manual of farming in twenty-eight books to be translated into Latin. It may have been concerned with intensive farming, particularly viticulture (the growing of vines) and animal husbandry.

To understand the work pattern of the ancient Romans, it is necessary to think back to a society without much mechanised power, whose town life was able to survive only if rural, agricultural areas could be organised to support it.

Early Romans, together with their sons (women did not do

---

Two Roman coins in the British Museum: (1) Hadrian and Britannia, (2) Antoninus Pius and Britannia. The figure of Britannia on the 50p piece and earlier coins is similar to these.

Roman sewer, York, discovered near Swinegate in 1972; height c 1m 50 (5ft). It dates from about AD 200, and went in part under a Roman street which had military housing (including water-closets) on one side and a bath-house on the other. The sewer drained into the river.

agricultural labour), worked hard on small subsistence plots, on which olives, vines and cereals were grown and a few animals kept. Latium and the Apennines are well suited to horticulture. But as Rome's dominions grew and lands like Etruria were

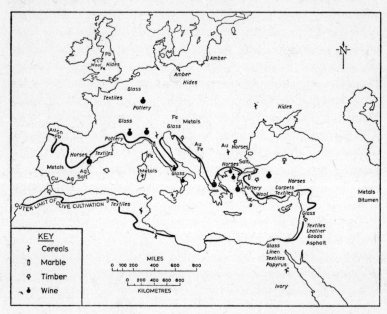

Fig 9    Simplified economic map of the Roman Empire

absorbed, large-scale farming with slave labour was introduced.

Cereals and legumes were grown in rotation, a procedure recommended by Virgil, Columella and the elder Pliny. The vine and the olive flourished in the Italian climate; Cato considered vine-growing the most profitable. In AD 91, to help Italian growers, Domitian decreed that vineyards in the provinces should be cut down by 50 per cent. Romans introduced viticulture into other countries, even into Britain, where however a law was in force until 281 prohibiting the sale of British wine. Before vines were planted, the land was ploughed, dug and prepared for irrigation. Then the vines were planted in trenches and supported, usually on small trees, after which

the vineyard was dug over three times and thoroughly irrigated
and manured. A model commercial vineyard in Italy described
by the elder Cato (234–149 BC) extended over 100 *iugera*
(25·2ha/62·3 acres), and was worked by sixteen slaves consisting
of one overseer and wife, ten farm-labourers, one oxherd, one
donkey-man, one willow-worker and one swineherd, and by
two oxen, two draft donkeys and two donkeys for the mill. But
it seems from the details of equipment that about thirty extra
helpers would be required at harvest time. 'The olive, queen
of trees', wrote Columella, 'requires the least expense.' It is
slow-growing, but can be combined with the growing of corn,
and this was done where conditions permitted. Olive oil was
used for cookery, as in Mediterranean areas today, for lighting,
embrocation and perfumery.

Italy remained self-sufficient within the peninsula for wine,
fruits, vegetables and meat. Many small-holders kept chickens
and bees; honey had the same importance in antiquity as sugar
today. But as cities grew, the corn supply for the urban population became a constant problem.

For grain imports Rome was dependent on Sicily (from
241 BC), the North African provinces (from 146 BC) and Egypt
(from 32 BC). The great majority of the corn was imported by
sea. Supplying the daily bread of Rome and the more populated
parts of Italy employed great numbers of slaves—in the province of origin and at Ostia and Rome—as well as the merchants and middlemen who handled the supplies. At Ostia the
quaestor supervised unloading, state officials measured the
corn, and it was sent to Rome, where the aediles distributed it.
In an emergency special commissioners were appointed. Gaius
Gracchus, tribune 123–122 BC, provided for a monthly ration
of corn to be sold on application at a low fixed price. The price
was further lowered by later politicians, and in 58 BC P. Clodius
made the ration free. Julius Caesar ruled that only 150,000 of
the poorest citizens could benefit from it, but Augustus raised
the number to 200,000. Free corn supply for legionaries was
started under Septimius Severus, and led to the imposition on
civilians in Italy and the provinces of a special tax (in kind)

for the purpose. Apart from regular cheap and free issues the market for corn and bread in Rome was not controlled, except that speculation was prohibited by law though perhaps not very effectively.

A great variety of corn mills has been preserved from antiquity. The earliest type used was a quern. The push-mill (*mola trusatilis*) had a millstone mounted on a long pole on a table and worked through an arc, as a man pushed and pulled at it alternately. The amount of slave power required was reduced when rotary mills were introduced. They are described by the elder Cato (c 160 BC) under the names of donkey-mill and Spanish mill, the latter probably a small do-it-yourself type. The usual type at Pompeii is in the shape of an egg-timer and was drawn by a donkey. Vitruvius describes a much more mechanised geared water mill; there is good reason to think that these were only rather gradually introduced in Rome.

Throughout the Empire, part of the land was privately owned; part, annexed after wars, was owned by the state, and divided up and leased to small-holders usually after careful survey. The practice of centuriation, ie dividing up into squares or rectangles land intended for apportionments, started as early as the fourth century BC and provided work for surveyors, who must have been numerous from the late first century BC. Land division was connected to a large extent with the foundation of colonies and the allocation of public domains (*ager publicus*). Traces of early centuriation can still be seen, for example, at Tarracina (Terracina), where in 329 BC 300 settlers were given small-holdings to rent. On all such holdings plots were allotted in *iugera* (1 *iugerum* = 0·252ha/0·623 acres). The number of *iugera* in a small-holding rose from 2 in the fourth century BC to 33⅓ or 50 in the first century BC. The original holding constituted a *heredium*, heritable plot, and the 'century' was so called because it usually contained 100 of these = 200 *iugera*. Large areas of centuriation are to be seen in the Po valley, Campania, Tunisia and elsewhere. With large distributions of public domains in the first half of the second century

BC, wealthy Roman landowners started to run *latifundia* like the large estates of Egypt under the Ptolemies, except that in Italy all work was done by slaves. Tiberius Gracchus (tribune 133 BC) started land reforms. He revived a law which had long been neglected, imposing a limit of 500 *iugera* of public land on each head of family, but added an extra allowance of 250 *iugera* for each child, up to a total maximum of 1,000. The land so confiscated was distributed to the poor in small-holdings. A later redistribution of land was of a different kind: from 43 BC the triumvirs appropriated lands in certain areas almost at random to allocate to their veterans. The original small unit arising from centuriation would be worked by a man and his family, but as the number of *iugera* grew, in most cases slaves would be involved.

Slaves were bought in the market; many of the unskilled farm workers were from barbarian countries. The overseer and his wife played a key part in the running of such farms. The overseer was expected to know or learn every aspect of farm work, so as to be able to direct the slaves, and to keep all necessary accounts; some thought he ought to be literate, others that he would be more likely to cook the books if he were. He had to see to it that the slaves were adequately clothed and fed, and that their health was attended to, and if necessary punish them. Crucifixion was applied for murder or conspiracy to escape. Columella mentions chaining and imprisoning of farm slaves in a cellar as a severe punishment for theft. But farm work in itself was regarded as a punishment for lazy town-slaves, who were sent to the country. Cato allocates the highest rations, 5lb a day, to workers in chain gangs who carried out heavy digging. The *vilica* (usually the overseer's wife) looked after wool workers and supervised other female slave activities, including the making of cheese and pickles.

As it was impossible to import meat from central and northern Europe, fish was the most important item of protein in the diet. Individual river fishermen on the Tiber were organised only for their special ceremonial games held on a fixed day, 6 June, near the river. As fish commanded a high price, there was plenty of competition for bringing it to market. Oyster-beds were cultivated on the Lucrine Lake and Lake Avernus, both north of the Gulf of Naples, and the stocks were carefully maintained. Evidence of fish-farming, mainly intended for the production of fish sauce (*garum*), has been found from the coasts of Spain, Morocco and Brittany. Fish tanks were often built near the sea, to keep fish alive and fresh; slaves were employed to attend to them. Sea fishing was only coastal. Sea fish were preferred to freshwater fish, so that owners of seaside villas let sea water into their fish-ponds. The best-known story about fishing is one of Cicero's. A Roman *eques* was a prospective buyer of a coastal villa near Syracuse. The owner, a Greek banker, asked him to a meal, and he could see relays of fishermen landing and presenting their catch to the owner. The Roman bought the villa at an inflated price, only to be told by a neighbour that it was a poor fishing area: 'In fact I wondered why all those fishing boats were here yesterday'. Legal comment would no doubt be *caveat emptor*, 'the buyer should beware'.

## MINING AND QUARRYING

The extractive industries, mining and quarrying, were able to be carried out on a large scale, in spite of lack of mechanisation, owing to a plentiful supply of slaves. The conditions in the mines were extremely poor; lighting was only by oil lamps, there were often fumes, ventilation was bad and conditions were cramped. Miners worked sometimes naked, sometimes wearing aprons, as shown on a relief found in Spain. Safety measures had to be imposed at the Vipasca mines in Spain during Hadrian's principate; among other provisions the damaging of props was made an offence. At the gold mines at Dolau Cothi, South Wales, pithead baths have been found. Gold was mined in north-west and southern Spain and in southern France, as well as at Dolau Cothi. It was also dredged from rivers, particularly in Asia Minor, Gaul and Spain. Silver was mined in large quantities in Spain and Asia Minor and to a smaller extent in Greece, Sardinia, Gaul and Britain. Lead was extracted from silver mines and used for pipes; in Britain the amount was limited by law, evidently to protect Spanish mines against financial loss. Copper was mined in Italy, Cyprus and Spain, and iron in many provinces.

Tin was worked more in Cornwall than elsewhere. Phoenicians or Carthaginians had been the first to exploit this area; indeed the search for minerals from the Bronze Age onwards was a main driving force towards discovery and ultimate settlement. The Greeks wrote of tin coming from the Cassiterides, 'tin islands', ie probably the Scilly Isles, which may have served as a trading post for Cornish tin. It was about 95 BC that P. Crassus, who may have been one of the governors in Spain, discovered the route from there to the Cassiterides, a secret long guarded by the Phoenicians.

Many people were employed in transport and manufacture of minerals. Gold and silver were used for jewellery, coins, tableware and plating. Coins were pressed between dies; under the Republic the mint at Rome was the sole source apart from military ones, while under Augustus Lugdunum (Lyons) and Alexandria were added, and later the number of mints was multiplied. Vases could be made of precious metal, and hammered out or moulded. Gold-leaf was much used for ornamentation. Bronze, a compound of copper and tin, was used for coins, kitchen vessels, tablets for inscriptions or maps, and also for statues, silver and bronze for statuettes. We have much evidence in museums of this work, and one can try to picture the workers who created them. Goldsmiths, silversmiths and gem engravers were mainly Greeks, some of whom, presumably including freedmen, had shops in the Via Sacra in Rome; these were lucrative employments. Iron was made by blacksmiths and craftsmen into weapons, agricultural implements, tools and ferrules. Others worked in bronze, lead, tin, iron and wood, or manufactured papyrus sheets.

Quarrying was hard work, carried out with much slave and convict labour. The ancients cut their stone blocks very exactly from the quarry face, so that where, as at Heliopolis (Baalbek,

Syria), unused monolithic columns survive, they are little larger in diameter than the finished product. From the mid first century BC marble was quarried at Luna, the modern Carrara, and it was also imported by sea from Greece and the Aegean, Asia Minor and North Africa. It was used for temples and other public buildings, for columns and other features of private houses, including internal decoration, and for statuary. Marble statuary, especially portraiture, was very often painted, though little of the decoration or colour has survived. Some cult dedications from quarries have been found and give us a clue to the conditions of work: for example, one at Luna records, 'The workshop set up this dedication, for our safety, to Hercules the helper.'

## POTTERY, GLASS AND TEXTILES

The most widespread manufacturing occupation, because of the wide availability of the raw material, the usefulness of the product and its fragile nature, has from very early times been the making of pottery. Potters, some of whom were slaves (even these might use individual potters' marks), worked in comparatively small potteries. The elder Pliny says that there was a corporation of potters from the reign of Numa. The influence of Greek pottery is to be seen on native ware from about 700 BC, and finds of pottery imported from Athens are frequent from the late sixth century BC. From then until the first century BC the main production areas are in the south of Italy, where the styles continued to be based on the Greek. But about 30 BC a distinctive Italian style is first introduced at Arretium (Arezzo), hence known as Arretine ware; this remained the chief centre of production for about 100 years. There were enormous factories of Samian ware in Gaul such as Lezoux in the Auvergne. As an indication of production, one factory in Gaul has graffiti recording the making of 500,000 pots. Potters also made earthenware, roof tiles, terracotta figurines (especially for religious offerings) etc. Imperial tile works were set up in the provinces; there was one at Pamber near Silchester. Distribution was carried out by pottery wholesalers.

Glassworks turned out window glass and a great variety of glass vessels. Glass-blowing was invented in the first century BC or earlier, and the mass production which followed resulted in many types of glass vessel largely replacing pottery. Manufacture of glass tended to move out of Italy into the provinces, especially north Gaul and Germany. In Britain glassworks have been found at Wilderspool, just across the Mersey from Warrington, and elsewhere.

The making of clothes is also one of the earliest occupations. Spinning was an activity on which Roman women of the early Republic spent an enormous amount of time, to the extent that epitaphs frequently use the phrase 'she made wool'. Spinning and weaving were an occupation not only of women at home but of female slaves in small factories, attached to and working primarily for houses of the wealthy and organised by the mistress of the house. Male labour was employed in weaving only in Egypt and not after the fourth century AD, when writers decry it as a sign of effeminacy. In Britain there is mentioned, about this time, an imperial textile factory at Venta, by which Winchester is probably meant, and no doubt there were factories distributed throughout the Empire. In addition to clothing, carpets, rugs and tapestries were woven. True silk was a luxury imported overland from China; garments made from it were only half silk before the third century AD. A substitute for it, wild (tussore) silk, was made into clothing on the island of Cos.

Rome was not a great centre of manufacture, since owners of country estates were able to muster more slave labour and space was necessary. The State itself competed in the provinces under the later Empire, and textiles, woodwork, metalwork, pottery and leatherwork were produced on public and private estates in Italy and the provinces.

## SHIPBUILDING

Service occupations must have been numerous to cope with transport and sales to feed such a widespread civilian population as well as the military and administrative personnel needed for keeping up such a large empire. The needs of these occupations created employment for other manufacturing workers, such as the makers of carts and ships to transport goods.

The heaviest and bulkiest items were carried by ship. Shipbuilding started as a branch of carpentry, since ships were all wooden, made mostly from conifers. The Romans learnt about the construction of warships in 260 BC from a stranded Carthaginian ship, just as we are able to learn about building methods, type of timber and use of ballast from the remains of the ship, almost certainly also Punic, stranded off Motya in west Sicily. In 205 BC, towards the close of the Second Punic War, Scipio induced Rome's allies in Etruria and Umbria to contribute towards shipbuilding. We are told that he received fir timber, iron, ships' canvas, ships' fittings, grain, weapons, armour, tools, baskets and hand-mills, and that the ships were launched only forty-five days after the timber had been received. Merchant ships, which had decks and cabins, were constructed less hastily and more carefully. Under the Empire, military and civilian harbours were separated, and with this separation warships came to be built in different areas from commercial vessels; Misenum on the Gulf of Naples was the main naval dockyard.

## SERVICES

The social standing of those engaged in services varied greatly. Personal services, of which there were many more than today, were carried out by slaves (for fullers see below). Certain professions or occupations were considered as ennobling, others as debasing. The important priesthoods, such as those of the

Pontifex Maximus and the augurs, tended to be monopolised by some of the older families, whereas local priesthoods or those attached to the emperor cult might be held by undistinguished men, in the latter case often freedmen. Army officers were mostly of senatorial or equestrian families except in time of emergency, while centurions made their way up from the ranks. Most legal experts under the Republic were senators; in the Empire they were either senators or men of high standing. The civil service was recruited from many varying walks of life. Appointments like the supervision of roads or of aqueducts went to senators, later to *equites*, whereas somewhat paradoxically the important ministerial posts under the early Empire, eg emperor's secretary (*ab epistulis*), supervisor of petitions (*a libellis*) etc, were held by freedmen.

Regular salaries for provincial governors were not instituted until the time of Augustus. As a result, under the late Republic (and even occasionally the Empire) provincial governors tended to enrich themselves at the expense of the provincials. Orators were able to circumvent a law, not rescinded until Claudius' principate, forbidding payment of a fee for defence. Thus when Cicero defended P. Sulla he received a large loan which he probably never paid back. Prosecution became particularly profitable under Tiberius, as a successful prosecution for treason was rewarded with one-quarter of the condemned man's property. Contracts for tax-collecting were most lucrative even if at times speculative.

At the other end of the scale the ordinary legionary, from the time of Julius Caesar to that of Domitian, received only 225 denarii a year with deductions for food, clothing and arms. Since the average cost of a slave was something like 500 denarii, and upkeep had to be considered, a legionary or veteran would never be able to afford one unless he had accumulated money from inheritance or permitted looting.

The literary world too may reasonably be included under the heading of services. Writers came from any social order: Julius Caesar, who wrote a book on grammar as well as accounts of his own military achievements, was of aristocratic birth and occupied the highest offices of state. Terence was a North African slave, freed in Rome; his name P. Terentius Afer indicates his origin. Of the most famous writers Cicero, Caesar, Seneca and Tacitus were of the senatorial class, Seneca's family being Spanish and Tacitus' evidently from Gaul or North Italy; Ovid was of equestrian family; Juvenal was evidently of a family well known at Aquinum, but he himself tells us nothing of its standing. Virgil's father was a local landowner in Cisalpine Gaul, Horace's father was a freedman, so that, at least in time of crisis, origin was no deterrent to success.

Schoolmasters came from all classes: there was the wealthy Quintilian, but there were also poor elementary school-teachers, including some slaves, and the same holds true of the medical profession. Artists were often Greeks, but never became as famous as their counterparts in Greece of the classical period. Architects in the west have mainly Roman names, in the east Greek; but this does not tell the whole story, since Aemilius Crescens of Pompeii, for example, was a freedman and could therefore be a Greek who had taken on his patron's name. Cicero employed a Greek slave, Cyrus, to build a library, and complained that when he suggested to Cyrus that the windows were too narrow Cyrus lectured him on optics. Vitruvius in his manual of architecture maintains that the architect should be master of almost all arts and crafts. Engineers and surveyors, both military and civilian, tended to be of humble origin, usually freedmen, in the earlier period. But some could certainly enrich themselves: C. Iulius Lacer, who built the famous Alcantara bridge over the upper Tagus, erected an imperial cult temple at his own expense, merely to celebrate its completion. The central span of the bridge is some 55m (60yd) above the river, and the size of the work, unparalleled for centuries after the fall of Rome, indicates the vast numbers of builders that must have been employed. Under the late Empire, surveyors improved their status by being called in as judges or arbitrators on land disputes and by being classified as teachers of geometry.

### FINANCE AND TRADING

Merchants enriched themselves particularly if they were willing to take risks with valuable cargoes in winter sailing conditions. Bankers operated individually or as small firms, making most of their money by loans. In 51 BC the Senate fixed a maximum of 12 per cent interest on loans, and rates from 6 per cent to 12 per cent were common. Unscrupulous creditors circumvented the maximum rate by lending in kind, eg two horses with promised repayment of three. Bankers also changed money: rates were fairly constant for Greek coins, more fluctuating for others. The term *publicani* referred in the Republic to tax-farmers, who were wealthy *equites*; in the Empire by less correct usage of the word it referred mostly to tax-collectors; the unpopular 'publicans' of the New Testament belong to this latter category.

The Romans did not have hotels of any size but inns, most of which were rather humble, run by *caupones*. The evidence from Pompeii shows that inns were plentiful there, two of them specially designed, others in single houses or pairs of houses, in several cases near gates of the town.

Shops could be set up by anyone enterprising enough. They were all small and run by a family, with help if required from their freedmen and slaves, and there was no equivalent of the chain-store. They were of the type common in the older parts of Mediterranean towns today, with no windows but with a door or shutter which represented the whole of the frontage, open to the road during the whole morning, and then, after a siesta break, for some hours of late afternoon. Butchers' shops in Rome, if we are to believe Livy, date back at least to the mid fifth century BC, since it was from one that Verginius snatched the knife that he plunged into his daughter Verginia, to save her from the clutches of the dictator Appius Claudius. The shelves of grocers' shops contained among other items many vessels of wine and oil, including a good number obtained from local growers; jars have been found at Pompeii with inscriptions like 'Quality Strained Sauce'. Bakers made their own bread, from wheat or emmet, on the premises. Lighting requirements were provided by several kinds of shops: candlestick maker, candle seller, oil merchant, lamp maker. Clothing, footwear and jewellery were made and sold in separate working shops. Blacksmiths and carpenters were among other small establishments common in cities. Barbers' shops were numerous, but we do not hear of women's hairdressers. Clothes were washed at home, but cleaned in fullers' shops by fullers (p 103) who washed them with water and soda, rinsed them, brushed them up, bleached them, treated them with fullers' earth and pressed them. Shopkeepers and craftsmen employed apprentices, mostly freedmen or slaves, whom they trained.

A typical middle-class townsman, doing nicely in the city but incapable of country work, is the Vulteius Mena whom Horace describes in *Epistles* i. 7. Philippus, consul 91 BC, was going home after work at the eighth hour when he spotted this auctioneer manicuring himself in an empty barber's booth. He invited him to dinner, made him a client, and by giving him 7,000 sesterces and lending him 7,000 induced him to buy a small plot. Although in the hope of quick profits he half-killed himself getting things going, nevertheless his sheep were stolen, his goats died of disease, his crop was unsatisfactory and his ox died from excessive ploughing. Finally he came back to his patron and implored him to let him return to his former occupation.

In addition to shops, there were stalls, markets and itinerant vendors. There was a fish-market in central Rome, where Plautus says members of dining-clubs used to congregate. Tanneries were situated out of town because a law banned them from the built-up area owing to their unpleasant smell.

Rome was the chief centre for foreign trade at every period, with Ostia and Puteoli (Pozzuoli) as its main ports. Most of the trade was with the provinces, but trade with areas outside the Roman Empire was also extensive. How did the Romans insure themselves against losses in such trading? The means ranged from religious propitiation to something akin to Lloyd's shipping insurance. Before starting on any major enterprise they took auspices to try to ensure the goodwill of the gods. They often promised an offering to a god, eg Neptune if they should come through dangerous seas. If one was superstitious one could consult an astrologer about propitious dates for sailing. But in addition the owner of a cargo could, as a form of insurance, take out what is known as a bottomry loan. A banker or friend would lend him money which had to be repaid with interest if the cargo arrived safely. Roman law stipulated that the creditor could demand as high a rate of interest as he chose for the actual period of the sea voyage, which from Ostia to Alexandria and back might be an average of forty days, but that ordinary commercial rates (6–12 per cent) applied for any period for which the loan continued after the end of the voyage.

The only state insurance of which we hear ended in a scandal. In 215 BC, during the Second Punic War, nineteen *publicani* belonging to three consortia contracted to supply food, clothing and supplies to the army and navy in Spain. They insisted on insurance by the State for all goods on board ship. Two years later they were tried and exiled for having loaded unseaworthy vessels with shoddy goods pretending they were sunk in a storm. No one dealt in fire insurance, and under the Republic there was no public fire brigade. This led to some sharp practice. M. Crassus (d 53 BC) organised a team of over 500 slave architects and builders in Rome. When a house caught fire, he and his slaves rushed up, and he offered to buy the house, and those on each side, cheap. If the owners agreed, they set to work putting out the fire and rebuilding; if not, they watched the fire and Crassus made lower offers. Augustus started an efficient fire service by instituting a corps of 7,000 *vigiles* as police and fire-fighters and dividing the city up into fourteen zones for this purpose.

## CONDITIONS OF LABOUR

There were no trade unions, only guilds (*collegia*), eg of smiths, carpenters, bakers, sailors. We do not hear that they ever made attempts to raise wages or ensure privileges for workers. The protest demonstration of silversmiths of Ephesus recorded in Acts 19. 23ff was exceptional. Partly because Rome was not a great manufacturing centre, and partly because many Romans despised all but the 'ennobling' occupations, the ability to earn a living was made more difficult when the city became overcrowded. The system of clientship, although resented by the poor, did help to relieve unemployment under the early Empire, when the State did very little to control or direct the labour market.

In later centuries we have some factual information on the economy. Trades, just like the civil service, tended to become more hereditary. Inflation, although not serious, was obviously beginning to make itself felt in Italy in Diocletian's reign, since in AD 301 he published the well-known edict setting up a prices and wages freeze. In its preamble he ascribed the rising prices to avarice and luxury. The schedule is extremely lengthy and detailed, and new fragments are discovered from time to time; some extracts are given in Table 2. Nevertheless it was not very long before the spiral resumed, and in the years 310–325 inflation in Italy was about sixfold.

The great difference between the ancient and modern labour market was the vast supply of slaves for so many centuries. The numbers of slaves used as construction workers were obviously very great, in the expansion of towns, in water control and in the construction of bridges, roads and harbours. Some idea of the speed of construction may be obtained from the waterworks of Rome carried out by Agrippa as aedile in 33 BC: he built the Aqua Virgo, repaired the other aqueducts, constructed 700 basins, 500 fountains and 139 distribution points, complete with 300 statues and 400 marble columns, all within one year. Many slaves must also have been needed for manual work on agricultural drainage and irrigation, especially in North Africa with its very small rainfall and consequent drought, where the digging of deep wells was indispensable to agricultural improvement.

Such a labour force clearly enabled enterprises to be carried out speedily (though official documents often took a long time to reach one office from another), effectively and cheaply. But it had a disadvantage in that there was little incentive to adopt new inventions. A fragment of the funeral monument of the Haterii in Rome shows a construction crane operated by a treadmill; but we are told that the emperor Vespasian discouraged similar inventions because they might have led to poverty among building workers.

Now Greeks of Alexandria, as evidenced by the works of Hero, were expert at inventing small mechanical devices. If Roman resources had been poured into research on the extension of some of these devices, it seems possible that power based on steam might have been developed. If Roman dominion had not been in decline from the third century AD, the comparative shortage of slaves from then on might have acted as an incentive to mechanical invention.

TABLE 2   EXTRACT FROM DIOCLETIAN'S EDICT ON PRICES

In AD 301 the emperor Diocletian published an edict on prices which was circulated among the cities of the Empire. Substantial fragments of it survive, and more fragments are found from time to time. The enclosed extracts are only a selection; varying prices refer to different types or qualities. The edict begins by drawing attention to the inflation, as mentioned above, then goes on to prescribe maximum prices for goods, services, wages and salaries.

1 *Food, drink*

| Item | Price in denarii | Quantity |
|---|---|---|
| Wheat | 100 | |
| Barley, rye | 60 | |
| Beans, crushed | 100 | Military peck |
| Beans, not crushed | 60 | (9l/c 15¼pt) |
| Lentils | 100 | |
| Rice, cleaned | 200 | |
| Wine | 8, 16, 24 or 30 | |
| Beer | 2 or 4 | Italian pint |
| Oil | 12, 24 or 40 | (0·546l/c 1pt) |
| Salt | 100 | Military peck |
| Honey | 8, 24 or 40 | Italian pint |
| Pork, lamb | 12 | |
| Beef, mutton, goat | 8 | Italian pound |
| Ham | 20 | (327g/c 9¾oz) |
| Lucanian sausage | 10 or 16 | |
| Pheasant | 125 or 250 | Each |
| Goose | 100 or 200 | |
| Chickens | 60 | Pair |
| Sea fish | 16 or 24 | Italian pound |
| River fish | 8 or 12 | |
| Cabbage, lettuce | 0·4 or 0·8 | |
| Eggs | 1 | Each |
| Peaches | 0·2 or 0·4 | |
| Cheese | 8 | Italian pound |

2 *Other Goods*

| Item | Price in denarii | Quantity |
|---|---|---|
| Oxhide, untanned | 300 or 500 | Each |
| Patrician shoes | 150 | Pair |
| Soldiers' boots, without nails | 100 | |
| Military saddle | 500 | Each |
| Large fir tree | 30,000 | 60ft × 6ft in girth |
| Oak, ash | 250 | 21ft × 3ft in girth |

| | | |
|---|---|---|
| Four-wheeled wagon with yoke, excluding ironwork | 1,500 | |
| Hooded cloak, Laodicean | 4,500 | Each |
| Dalmatic (tunic), unmarked | 2,000 | |
| African cloak | 500 | |
| Sheeting, third quality, from Laodicea | 5,250 | |
| Sheeting, coarse, for common people or slaves | 800–1,750 | Web |
| Towelling, Gallic, third quality | 820 | |

3 *Wages, salaries*

| Occupation | Denarii | Unit |
|---|---|---|
| Farm labourer | 25 | 1 day, with keep |
| Stone mason, carpenter | 50 | 1 day |
| Mosaic worker | 50 or 60 | 1 day |
| Barber | 2 | 1 customer |
| Scribe | 20 or 25 | 100 lines |
| Elementary teacher | 50 | 1 month, per boy |
| Teacher of rhetoric | 250 | 1 month, per pupil |
| Tailor, for work on hooded cloak | 40 or 60 | 1 cloak |
| Linen weaver | 20 or 40 | 1 day, with keep |
| Fuller, for new hooded cloak of Laodicea wool | 175 | Cleaning of 1 cloak |

4 *Transport costs*
(a) *Sea*

| From | To | Denarii | Unit |
|---|---|---|---|
| ? Libya | Sicily | 6 | |
| ? Libya | Thessalonica | 18 | Military peck |
| ? Libya | Spain | 10 | |
| Nicomedia | Rome | 18 | |

(b) *Land*

| | | |
|---|---|---|
| 1,200lb wagon load | 20 | denarii per mile |
| Donkey load | 4 | |

# 7

## *How They Learnt and Wrote*

ROMAN education during the classical period was founded on the framework of Greek education. But whereas the Greeks taught not only reading, writing, arithmetic, poetry, rhetoric and philosophy, but gymnastics and music, the Romans omitted gymnastics and put less value on musical training. Since Greeks had led the way in every subject and had put their educational faith in literature, rhetoric and philosophy, Romans always looked on their predecessors in these fields with respect, and aimed at being 'learned in both languages'.

Some time after 272 BC Livius Andronicus, a Greek from Tarentum, came to Rome as a prisoner of war. When he had gained his freedom he translated Homer's *Odyssey* and a number of tragedies (the first in 240 BC) into Latin verse. The *Odyssey* translation was so popular that, despite being in the rough and primitive Saturnian metre, it was still used in schools 200 years later. Homer was regarded as the greatest poet of all time, and the *Iliad* and *Odyssey* were taught very thoroughly in all schools. Particular attention was paid to Greek grammar. One of the first lecturers on that subject in Rome was Crates of Mallos, who went there about 168 BC as an envoy from Pergamum. He was keen to learn about the achievements of Roman engineering, but had the misfortune to break his leg when examining the Cloaca Maxima, and he gave his lectures during his convalescence. Greek was also the *lingua franca* of the Near East, Sicily and south Italy, and young

Romans regarded it not only as an academic accomplishment but as a practical asset to have a fluent command of Greek.

On this topic there is an interesting suggestion by Quintilian (M. Fabius Quintilianus), from whose *Institutio Oratoria*, a complete manual of education for the Roman orator, we gather valuable information. He was born in Spain, but for many years from about AD 55 taught rhetoric in Rome. Writing towards the end of the first century AD, he approved of Roman boys beginning their studies with Greek, since they were bound to acquire fluency in Latin in any case. But certainly Latin language and literature were not on that account neglected.

In early times boys were taught by their mothers until the age of seven, then by their fathers; for example, in senatorial families they accompanied them at their business in the city, learning from them among other things something of law and of the use of weapons. When they were aged sixteen, they were apprenticed to some well-known Roman, after which they went to do military service. This apprenticeship and military training continued in classical times; and in some noble families the system of education by the parents persisted right down to the Empire.

### ELEMENTARY SCHOOLS

It was probably only from the time of the Punic Wars onwards that formal education became customary. Three stages of education could be pursued in Rome and other places in Italy (the fourth, as will be seen, was normally in Greek lands): elementary, literary and rhetorical. The elementary teacher was known as *litterator*. The customary age of elementary education (not compulsory, but almost universal for sons and daughters of Roman citizens) was from seven to twelve, though Quintilian thought seven too late for an able boy to start. Wealthier families employed a slave called the *paedagogus* to accompany their children to and from school; our word 'pedagogue' comes from this, but only by a shift of meaning. The schoolroom was usually a very simple one, with a chair for the master and benches for the children. The subjects at this level were mainly reading, writing and simple arithmetic, but the reading and writing were of Greek as well as of Latin. Wax writing-tablets were either provided by the schools or brought in satchels. The counting-board (*abacus*) was used for arithmetic, much as in Japan today. An alphabet served to teach the shapes and sounds of letters; early ones of twenty-one letters survive. There were twenty-three letters of the classical Latin alphabet; I and U(V) were used as consonants as well as vowels, the consonantal U taking the place of our W, and J developed later from consonantal I. Just as in Greek schools, syllables were taught before words. Only occasionally do we hear of something like visual aids; there were, for example, cartoons that told the story of the Trojan War, and paintings of places in Italy. Most writers in antiquity speak of drudgery and learning by rote; but Quintilian, an idealist as well as a practical teacher of rhetoric, was keen that schooling should be made entertaining, with question and answer and a suitable measure of praise where deserved.

As to the arithmetic, Horace criticises it for being too closely linked with commerce; thus fractions, by a system derived from Greek education, were painfully taught as part of the duodecimal monetary system, eg $\frac{5}{12} + \frac{1}{12}$as $= \frac{1}{2}$as, $\frac{5}{12} - \frac{1}{12}$as $= \frac{1}{3}$as. The Roman system of numbers, I = 1, V = 5, X = 10, L = 50, C = 100, D = 500, ∞ = 1,000 (or M as abbreviation of *mille*), was no more easily accommodated than the usual Greek system (A = 1, B = 2 etc) to multiplication or division. Intermediate numbers could be expressed by addition or subtraction, eg IIII or IV = 4. Thousands could be expressed by placing a bar over the appropriate numbers.

Discipline tended to be strict in the earlier stages, and frequent punishment of boys for bad work as well as for bad behaviour was regular, though disapproved of by Quintilian. The usual method was to hit them on the hand with a rod (*ferula*). Work started very early in the morning, often before dawn. The pay brought by the boys whom Horace mentions was 8 asses a month (a legionary in his time received 10 asses a day).

The level of literacy varied enormously. By the fourth century AD, according to Vegetius, army recruits were often too ignorant to keep the books. It is difficult to assess the level in classical times: Pompeii, where many graffiti are in bad Latin, was influenced by Oscan and Greek, while literary texts either aim at good Latin or parody vulgar speech. In general the impression is of very different levels of attainment.

Carcopino maintained that the elementary schools were in every way a hopeless failure. Granted that most of them did not live up to Quintilian's ideals, they did at least attempt to inculcate something of Roman *gravitas* and, like Victorian schools, give their pupils suitable maxims to remember. Thus handwriting might be taught with the versified sayings of Publilius Syrus, such as:

> *A miser causes his own misery.*
> *A good man's anger is no light affair.*
> *Man's life-span is a loan and not a gift.*

Education for girls was customary at the lowest level. A certain number went on beyond, and in particular girls of senatorial families were often given a very good education. Cornelia, mother of the Gracchi, was a most cultured woman who, when her husband died (154 BC), personally educated her children and at the same time managed her estate. Sulpicia, daughter of Cicero's friend Servius Sulpicius Rufus, wrote elegiac poetry which was both learned and passionate. Learned women were familiar enough to be joked about: Juvenal, who disliked many features in the character of the women of Rome, says he loathes the woman who keeps quoting Homer and Virgil.

## LITERATURE AND MATHEMATICS IN
### MIDDLE SCHOOLS

The next stage was that of the *grammaticus*, who might be said to correspond to the teacher in the Middle School. He taught mainly literature; he did also teach grammar, but this, despite the name, was not his prime task. The father of the poet Statius was a *grammaticus*, who at his school in Naples in the mid first century AD attracted pupils from far and wide. He was particularly noted for his excellent renderings of Homer into Latin. A century earlier the poet Horace was given a good education by a *grammaticus* in Rome. His father refused to send him to the local school at Venusia in southern Italy, where hefty sons of centurions went, and sent him to Lucius Orbilius Pupillus in Rome, who presumably charged more. Orbilius used as a translation of the *Odyssey* the old one by Andronicus, and Horace remembered him for the whacks he gave during the *Odyssey* lessons.

Under the Republic not only Homer but many other Greek poets were recommended for reading. But in 26 BC the poetry of Virgil, recognised as great from the beginning, was introduced into schools. Following this Horace and other poets and Greek and Latin prose authors were introduced into the curriculum. The normal method consisted of explanation by the master, reading by the pupils, then either question and answer or a summary by the master. Adults as well as children were in the habit of reading aloud. Accuracy of texts had to be checked by the master since there were good, bad and indifferent copies. Some schools may have had only one copy of each book for each form, while others would have a supply of the more regularly used books for each pupil. Papyri from Egypt dating from the fourth century AD, with their Greek 'cribs' of Virgil and other poets, suggest the latter procedure. Geometry and more advanced arithmetic seem to have been taught at this stage. The writers on geometry were Greeks, especially Euclid

(c 300 BC). From the agricultural manual (AD 60–65) of Columella, we can judge that most Romans studied just so much
geometry as would help them with the practical running of an
estate. There are likely to have been some examinations attached
to general education, since we hear of obligatory 'displays' in
Greek schools in Alexandria.

## RHETORIC IN UPPER SCHOOLS

The third stage, which might be said to correspond to the
Upper School, though the age at which it was started varied
considerably, was rhetorical training. The elder Cato (234–149
BC) had put forward as an ideal 'the good man skilled in
speaking'. In Rome, just as with the Greeks, success in public
life depended in large measure on being able to speak well in
public. Admittedly in early times Romans were suspicious of
men who claimed to be able to put just the right words into
anyone's mouth, and in 161 BC rhetoricians were expelled from
the city. But within twenty years of that date we hear of a
Roman acquiring a smoothness of diction that rivalled the
Greeks, and before long rhetoric had gained an established
place in the curriculum. By *declamatio* was meant a series of
exercises on themes invented by the rhetorician or handed down
from his predecessors, themes such as had been used in Greek
cities from the third century BC. In Cicero's time they were
divided into (1) abstract, general themes, (2) particular themes
related to a situation. As examples of the general theme we have
—'Should one marry?'—and—'Should one embark on political
activity?' In dealing with these themes, young orators were
trained to bring in their knowledge of philosophy; thus marriage
could be held to be harmful to philosophical contemplation, or
the Stoic philosopher could advocate active participation in
politics while the Cynic (in some ways foreshadowing the hippy)
could argue for complete detachment. For the detailed theme
we have—'Should Carthage be allowed to ransom its prisoners
of war?' and—'Should the younger Scipio Africanus, because

of his achievements, be allowed to become consul under the legal age?' For this type of theme a knowledge of history, politics and law was most desirable; and by this means the rhetorical schools prepared young men for political and legal oratory. The five points on which the orator had to concentrate were (1) the finding of suitable material, (2) arrangement, (3) diction, (4) remembering what was appropriate, (5) delivery. Under this last heading stress was laid on tone and gesture. Each type of speech, eg the congratulatory address or the funeral oration, had its set features which were carefully taught.

### SIMULATION TECHNIQUES

Under the Empire, or perhaps even earlier, the exercises of the rhetorical schools developed into (1) *suasoriae*, speeches of advice, (2) *controversiae*, set debates. In *suasoriae*, by a type of simulation akin to the latest game technique, the speaker had to imagine himself in a mythological or historical situation, arguing for or against a particular course of action. Thus one of the famous stories of Greek mythology was that Agamemnon, commander of the Greek expedition against Troy, was persuaded by the priest Calchas to sacrifice his daughter Iphigenia in order to placate the goddess Artemis and obtain a favourable wind for sailing. The speaker could aim at 'persuading' Agamemnon not to adopt this terrible remedy. Or, an example which Juvenal gives in his first satire, he could pretend to advise the dictator Sulla (who died about 180 years before Juvenal was writing) to lay down his powers and enjoy a quiet retirement. The *controversiae*, on the other hand, were debates set in the framework of an invented story and governed by legal conditions which were sometimes rather arbitrary. Some of the themes remind us of those of the New Comedy and its Roman adaptations: thus we have stories of girls seized by pirates when they are young and reunited with their parents only when they have grown up. An example from the elder Seneca is:

*A man captured by pirates wrote to his father asking to be ransomed. He was not successful. The pirate chief's daughter said he must swear to marry her if he was freed. He took this oath. She left her father and accompanied the young man, who married her and returned to his father. A childless heiress then came into the picture. The father ordered the son to divorce the pirate's daughter and marry the heiress. When the young man refused, the father disinherited him.*

The discussion is on whether the father, granted his powers as *paterfamilias*, had any right to act as he did. Another example:

*A Vestal Virgin, condemned for inchastity, called for help to the goddess Vesta before being thrown down from the Tarpeian rock. When she was thrown down she survived. She was brought back for punishment.*

Here the question is how, if at all, she should be punished. The intended object was to supply a sufficient framework to make words come naturally. It has been shown that as a preparation for the law-courts under the Empire, as with today's speeches at bar dinners, these exercises were not as unrealistic as would seem at first sight. Another parallel today is to be found in toastmaster courses, which aim at equipping one to make an after-dinner speech. Unfortunately one actual result was to encourage speakers to outdo each other in pithy catch-phrases, and to introduce 'purple patches' of description. Here is one on sudden deaths, drawing on the cycle of nature, 'All the birds that fly, all the fishes that swim, all the animals that run about find their graves in our bellies. You ask why we die suddenly: it is by deaths that we live.' Historical examples were encouraged:

*Who was Marius if we take a look at his ancestors? He was of low birth. The precedent for all his consulships lay in the man himself. If Pompey had been helped up by portraits [literally wax busts, imagines] of ancestors, would anyone have called him The Great?*

*Rome had Servius as a king* [servus = *slave*]: *among his virtues what is more famous than the humility of his name?*

These *controversiae* and *suasoriae* persisted right through the Empire: Ennodius speaks of a rhetorical school at Mediolanum (Milan) about AD 500 having the thankless son, the tyrannicide, or subjects from Greek mythology as its themes.

The rhetoricians' method was based on teaching the five points summarised above. At first the trainee would be given preliminary exercises, then he would be introduced to the forms of *declamatio* mentioned. Stress was laid, in training for law-court speeches, in appealing to the emotions and interests of the jury, by the tone of one's speech, by gesture, by blackening the character of opponents and so forth. The system did not go unchallenged. Petronius made a character say: 'It is parents who deserve criticism for not letting their children benefit from strict discipline . . . They drive immature schoolboys into the law-courts, and force that noble faculty, eloquence, on still struggling children.'

### OTHER HIGHER EDUCATION, LAW AND PHILOSOPHY

The fourth stage of higher education, which corresponds roughly to the university level, consisted mainly of three branches: Roman law, Greek oratory and philosophy. It is in the sphere of law that Rome made perhaps her greatest contribution to education. The usual method of instruction under the Republic and the early Empire was for young men to be apprenticed to a legal expert. Cicero gained his legal training, which was very extensive, from two famous jurists. By the second century AD we find regular law schools set up to perform the same function.

Greek oratory was taught especially at Athens and Rhodes, and young Romans often combined it with philosophy. The chief centres of philosophical learning were Athens, Rhodes, Pergamum, Alexandria (more noted for mathematics and science) and the Bay of Naples. Alexandria was also famous for its great Greek library built up under the Ptolemies. The chief philosophical schools operating in Roman times were the Stoic, Epicurean, Academic and Peripatetic. Of these the Stoic became by at least the first century AD the most influential, because its belief in the active, involved life appealed to the Roman sense of citizenship. Greek philosophical and rhetorical schools, with their intense hatred of tyranny, inspired Brutus and his followers to assassinate Julius Caesar, and Stoics under the Empire to embark on active opposition to the Imperial system.

The best picture of a student's life in classical times comes from the pen of a famous man's son. Cicero sent his son Marcus to Athens as a pupil of the Greek philosopher Cratippus, whom Caesar had made a Roman citizen. Marcus wrote to his father's secretary, Tiro:

> *I have no doubt, my dear Tiro, that the reports about me now are pleasing and what was hoped for. I shall see to it that this new-born reputation of mine gets bigger every day. So you may confidently be my publicity agent as you promised. The mistakes of my youth have brought me so much distress and torment that I want them out of my hearing as well as out of my mind . . . Cratippus and I are very close; I am more like a son than a pupil of his. I enjoy his talks and appreciate his pleasant company. I spend whole days with him, and often part of the night: I ask him to dine with me as often as possible . . . I never let Bruttius out of my sight. His way of life is frugal and strict, his company most pleasant. His jokes are linked with his study of literature and daily discussions. I have rented him digs near mine, and am helping his lack of funds with my mediocre resources.*

## TECHNICAL EDUCATION

Technical education, although obviously thorough and very important, was never given quite its due recognition in the

Roman system. Cicero (*De Officiis* i. 150–51) classes tax-collectors, bankers, manual labourers, retail traders, mechanics, cooks, fishermen, perfumers and dancers under vulgar employment. So if a profession was to be esteemed, it had to establish its links with liberal (gentlemanly) pursuits. There were specialist teachers of music, mathematics and science, who supplemented the general instruction in such subjects offered by the *grammatici*. Music and gymnastics were not accorded the high place in the curriculum that they had in Greece. Medicine and architecture were highly esteemed by most, though individual doctors and architects came in for criticism. Vitruvius, writing in the first century AD, is at pains to outline the large number of related subjects that the student of architecture should master: astronomy, cosmology, geometry, history, law, medicine, music, painting and philosophy. A case had to be built up for the inclusion of a subject like land surveying in the liberal arts. It required the learning of geometry, astronomy and Roman law, but also claimed to be descended from Etruscan religious practice. In medicine we hear of Asclepiades of Prusa in Bithynia (first century BC) as the first great teacher in Rome: he believed in Democritus' atomic theory, taken up by Epicurus and Lucretius, which, in dismissing the theory of humours is much nearer modern physical theory than any other speculations in antiquity. Galen of Pergamum, who went to Rome in AD 162, achieved fame as a teacher of medicine as well as a writer, researcher and practitioner. A skill much taught under the Empire was shorthand, a knowledge of which led to promotion in the civil service. A papyrus from Egypt, dated AD 155, mentions a young slave for whom his master paid a shorthand teacher on the understanding that he would be fully taught within two years.

## FINANCING OF EDUCATION

The State at first interested itself in education only to the extent of expelling foreign teachers who were regarded as undesirable. But Julius Caesar offered Roman citizenship to Greek teachers, so that a number came to Rome. Vespasian appointed teachers of Greek and Latin rhetoric in Rome to positions almost like those of modern professors, with state-paid salaries: the first to teach Latin rhetoric at a 'public school' in Rome was Quintilian. Trajan provided free education for nearly 5,000 poor children of citizens in Rome, and the younger Pliny was moved to follow his example on a smaller scale at Comum (Como). We read (iv. 13): 'Recently, when I was in my home area, the teenage son of a fellow-townsman came to pay his respects to me. I said "Are you at school?" "Yes." "Where?" "At Mediolanum [Milan]." "Why not here?" His father, who had brought the boy, said: "Because we have no teachers here." ' Pliny then, according to his letter carefully prepared for publication, launched into a powerful plea for education nearer home, adding that being childless he was prepared to put up one-third of any sum the parents thought necessary for founding a local school. We learn from inscriptions that he gave money, among other objects, for scholarships to poor children in the town and for the foundation and upkeep of a public library. Hadrian founded an institute called the Athenaeum, which organised lectures and literary readings. Marcus Aurelius set up four teaching posts in Athens, one in rhetoric and four in philosophy. The result of this state activity was to open up secondary education, at least in some areas, to the poorest children, and to establish the equivalent of professors, but not universities as such.

In the later Empire too there were more students in Rome and Athens than elsewhere; other centres were Alexandria, Constantinople, Carthage and several places in Asia Minor and Gaul. Augustine praises the students of Rome as orderly in comparison with those in Carthage. At Athens the system of many 'professors' but no university sometimes resulted in cut-throat competition and a sort of tug-of-war: freshers who landed at the Piraeus were seized by rival gangs of students who tried to enrol them with their own teachers. In Rome an edict of AD 370 provided that all students and pupils from distant parts should carry a letter of authorisation; should register at the city prefect's office, which checked on them monthly and could expel them; and were not allowed to stay after the age of twenty. This was the commonest age to cease study, but at Berytus (Beirut) the upper age limit was twenty-five.

### BOOKS AND WRITING

Two types of writing material were used in schools. One was the wax tablet, used for exercises and notes. This was a pair or series of wooden-framed rectangles with waxen inner sections. The two or more frames were bound together with leather thongs. The name for the tablets was *codicilli*, diminutive of *codex*, which literally means 'trunk of tree', 'block of wood', or *cerae*, plural of *cera*, 'wax'. For writing on the wax tablet a pointed stilus was used. The writing could be rubbed off by using the head end of the stilus. A tablet could also be given a white surface to enable it to be written on with ink.

For more permanent purposes students and pupils used books copied out by slaves, though fewer books were in use than today and there was more learning of passages by heart from the master. The Latin for 'book' is *liber*, which literally means the bark of a tree; this had been one of the earliest materials to take writing. Under the Republic and the early Empire the normal form of book was a papyrus roll, whereas by the late Empire the fashion had changed to the parchment or vellum codex, more or less corresponding in manuscript to our book form. There was admittedly some overlap, since the use of material (papyrus or parchment) did not necessarily tie up with the type of book (roll or codex); but to simplify we may consider only these two forms.

Papyrus (*Cyperus papyrus*) is a reed with a thin triangular stem. In ancient times it grew abundantly on the shores of the Nile; now it is rare. The pith of the stem was cut into strips which were made to face alternate directions; it was moistened on top with water and a little glue, a further set of strips was placed on top at right angles, and the two were stuck together by being pressed. This criss-cross, when trimmed, gave a sheet of writing material. The next procedure was to glue the sheets together to form a roll, which was then wound round a wooden stick, sometimes with bosses at each end to help turning. The roll was called *volumen*, from *volvo* = revolve, hence our 'volume'. It was the practice to divide long works into books, and where the roll system was used each book normally occupied one roll.

In classical times the scribe wrote in columns at right angles to the length of the roll. The exception was despatches under the late Republic, which were written parallel to the length. As with Greek, there was not necessarily any division between words, though sometimes we find dots between each word; and punctuation was rather haphazard. For literary texts the normal form of script during the classical period was what is known as Rustic Capitals (Fig 10 (a)). For rough notes a cursive hand, quicker but much harder to read (Fig 10 (b)), was considered sufficient. A further style—Uncials—was a feature of the late Empire (Fig 10 (c) ).

Instead of papyrus, parchment or vellum could be used. The Greek term for parchment is *pergamene*, from Pergamum in Asia Minor. The elder Pliny says that it was invented there (the date implied is between 197 and 182 BC), when the Egyptian king Ptolemy V prohibited the export of papyrus. The statement could be true if applied to a new process. Untreated leather had been used as a writing surface from earliest times; but this was specially prepared. Skins of cattle, sheep and goats were washed, scraped and rubbed with pumice and chalk. Then, if they were intended for use in the codex form of book, the sheets were bent in two and gathered in quires (*quaterni* = four each). The final process consisted of sewing and sticking the quires into position within a tough parchment cover. The use of vellum codices is mentioned in the first century AD, but it was probably only with the greater need for legal and Christian works in the third century AD that they came into prominent use. Clearly the book form is more practical than the roll form when one wants merely to turn to a particular

CERVICIBVS·ASTIDE·MOLLEM·
LABITVRIN·SOMNVM·
PERCVLIT[ ]FLATV·BREVIS·

a

b

## FACTUM EST AUTEM CUM
## TURBAE INRUERENT INEUM

c

Fig 10   Comparative styles of handwriting; (b) begins Cn. Pompeio
Grospho Grospho

reference. With a papyrus roll (normally written only on one side) the reader had to keep turning the ends as he went along. If he had reached the end and then wanted to copy out a passage from the middle, he would have to roll the *volumen* back with some difficulty until the right passage was reached.

Whereas the stilus was the writing instrument for wax tablets, the instrument for papyrus and parchment was the quill pen, which in various forms lasted right down to the nineteenth century. The ink was normally black, made of soot and glue, somewhat akin to our printer's ink. This is far more permanent than either fountain-pen or biro ink, and explains why few ancient manuscripts have become wholly illegible through passage of time. To rub out on papyrus the Romans applied a sponge, whereas with parchment the only effective method was scraping with a knife.

## THE BOOK TRADE

Before the invention of the printing press, it was inevitable that the copying out of books took a long time. Large-scale copying was almost entirely done by slaves, and authors and publishers (the same as booksellers) paid high prices for well educated ones. We know something of the process of publication in the case of Cicero's works. He frequently dictated to his secretary Tiro, who took his words down in shorthand and arranged the works for publication. Then many copies of the original manuscript were made, either by booksellers' slaves or by those of his friend T. Pomponius Atticus. Copies were sold by the booksellers, who also dealt in second-hand books. The quality and price of books varied according to their appearance, so that old school-books blackened by candles would be cheap, while a new and attractive volume, especially if it had knobs on the cylinder and a handsome red cover, could be expensive. Martial tells us that Book XIII of his epigrams (AD 84–5) was sold by a bookseller for 4 sesterces (16 asses). There was no system of copyright, so that an author, having once sold his manuscript to the bookseller, did not profit by large sales. There were no fixed prices for books, and booksellers' profits depended on supply and demand.

In booksellers' shops it was the custom to hang books on pillars, but in libraries roll books could either be stacked singly on shelves or grouped in cylindrical boxes, which were labelled and stored on shelves or in cupboards. The problem of bulk storage occurred with collections of the more lengthy Greek and Latin works. The Greek philosopher Chrysippus is said to have written 705 works. As an example of the longer Latin work, Livy's history of Rome originally occupied 142 books. Even if a collector could afford all the Greek and Latin works in which he was interested, he might have difficulty in finding space for them. So means were looked for to meet this problem. Martial mentions, among presents given to friends, some vellum books in codex form of which he writes:

> *For Livy's bulk my shelves are not designed:*
> *Accept him in some tiny skins confined.*

Either this was an abridgement or it was written in very small letters. If the latter, it can only have been an experiment, since we do not know that the ancients had magnifying-glasses, without which the reading of small lettering would be trying to the eyes. But when the vellum codex with larger letters came in, this did solve the storage problem. The writing was regularly on both sides, and there were no central cylinder or turning-knobs to take up space, so that much economy of shelving was achieved. Thus established, the codex led, with the much later invention of printing and the introduction of paper, to the modern book.

### THE LATIN LANGUAGE

'Latin' means, in origin, the language of Latium, the area mainly south of the Tiber. As Rome expanded, the use of Latin expanded correspondingly. It became the official language of the Empire, but in Greek-speaking lands Greek retained its pre-eminence in all other spheres.

Latin was one of a number of Italic dialects which, unlike Etruscan, were Indo-European, akin to Greek, Germanic and Celtic. Two other Italic dialects were Oscan and Umbrian, which continued to be talked in classical times: Oscan inscriptions have been found at Pompeii. The Italic dialects show a variation between p and q forms similar to that found in Celtic. Latin, for example, has *quinque* for 'five', while Oscan had *pompe*. The closest dialect to Latin was Faliscan, in which we find, for example, this sentence, *foied uino pipafo, cra carefo,* 'today I shall drink wine, tomorrow I shall do without,' which in Latin would be *hodie uinum bibam, cras carebo*.

There seem to have been three stages in accentuation: (1) a

pitch accent in the ancestor of Latin, (2) an early tendency for the accent to be a stress one on the first syllable, (3) in classical Latin, in words of more than one syllable the accent was usually on the last syllable but one if this syllable was long, but went back to the last syllable but two if not. One result of this development was that the values of vowels changed. Some of these changes are evident by comparison with Greek; others occur within Latin itself, eg:

| Simple verb | Meaning | Compound | Meaning |
| --- | --- | --- | --- |
| capio | take | accipio | accept |
| caedo | cut | occido | kill |

Latin, like all older Indo-European languages, is highly inflected, having three genders and six cases. The advantage of this is that word-order can be very flexible, the disadvantage is that the popular language is more likely to diverge from the written language.

A common construction of literary Latin was the ablative absolute, which arose out of the instrumental and sociative uses (often 'with' + noun in English), such as *Numa regnante* 'while Numa was reigning' (*regnante* being ablative of *regnans* present participle of *regno*). Another feature of the literary language was subordination by clauses, often having a verb in the subjunctive. As a result, the spoken language, such as we find in the early comedies of Plautus and Terence, in some of Cicero's letters, and in parts of Petronius' novel, remained simple in syntax, while the literary language became more complicated. The rhetorical type of education under which most Romans were brought up had the effect of keeping the two apart, by aiming at embellishment and at a correctness which the colloquial language had often discarded. Thus Vespasian, noted for his countrified speech, is reported to have said on his deathbed *Vae, puto deus fio*, 'Oh dear, I think I'm becoming a god', for the last two words of which a more literary Roman would have substituted *me deum fieri*, 'that I am becoming a god', using the accusative and infinitive construction for reported speech. That was one of a number of constructions that never gained a firm foothold in vulgar Latin.

As a vehicle for poetry and prose, Latin underwent various improvements before it could be said to be adequate. Its early vocabulary was simple and geared mainly to concrete things. It borrowed words from Etruscan, and had a vocabulary useful for everyday life but of little use for such a subject as philosophy. The introduction in 240 BC of translations from Greek poetry lent a more literary look to the language. Whereas Q. Fabius Pictor at the end of the third century BC wrote his history of Rome in Greek, later historians whose language was Latin wrote in that language. Terence, who started life in Rome as a North African slave, by his smooth verses paved the way for classical versification. In the late Republic Lucretius tried the bold experiment of expressing Greek philosophy in Latin hexameter verse, for which purpose he had to invent a number of new terms and complained of the poverty of Latin to express abstract thought. Cicero not only forged a model of classical prose-writing, inventing terms like *qualitas*, based on the Greek, which has given us the word 'quality', but also writing hexameter verse which sometimes sounded flat and unintentionally comic but which achieved a greater measure of polish than any previous writers. It was left to Virgil fully to perfect Latin poetic diction, and to the writers of Silver Latin (first–second century AD) to elaborate the literary language with rhetorical embellishment. When Christian Latin came in, it aimed at simple wording which could be understood by the humblest reader, and at literal translations from Hebrew and Greek, which sounded odd in the ear of an educated Roman (thus *orare* could mean 'pray' in classical Latin, but not in a religious sense) but which were well suited to their particular object. As Latin was used for official purposes in the Eastern Empire as well as the Western, it was the language of Justinian's legal Digest. In the Middle Ages its use by monastic communities contributed greatly to the transmission of classical learning to posterity.

# 8

## *How They Spent Their Leisure Time*

THE Latin for 'leisure' is *otium*, and its opposite, *negotium* (*necotium*), means 'business'. The earlier word of the two was clearly *otium*, both because of the formation of the word and because business does not play much part in primitive societies. Indeed the idea of leisure as something desirable was nearly always present at the back of Romans' minds; though the younger Pliny disliked leisure, so *otiosus* (adjective from *otium*) could convey something undesirable to him. And a Pompeii graffito may be rendered: 'No room for leisured people here: go away, loiterer.' Sometimes leisure involved going from Rome into the country and taking things quietly. But in Rome itself there were many leisure pursuits which could be followed.

### HOLIDAYS AND PUBLIC GAMES

Roman society was developed, with the aid of slave labour, to the extent that in the city all classes, apart perhaps from slaves, were able to enjoy plenty of leisure. The great majority of serious work in Rome took place during the morning, so that the afternoon hours of each day were free for leisure activities. Moreover, although there was in classical times no such thing as a week or weekend, the number of festival days in the year was already high by the late Republic and was constantly on the increase. Just as the word 'holiday' means 'holy day' and points to the religious association, so the *ludi* (games) of classical Rome, which accounted for the majority of the holidays, were with few exceptions associated with some deity. Increases in the number of these arose owing to the celebration of victories or the commemoration of emperors' achievements. The following table shows the extent of the *ludi* in Rome under the early Empire:

| Month | Number of days | Festival | Date of institution | Patron deity |
|---|---|---|---|---|
| April | 7 | Ludi Megalenses | 204 BC | The Great Mother |
| April | 8 | Cerealia | Before 202 BC | Ceres |
| April–May | 6 | Floralia | 173 BC | Flora |
| July | 8 | Ludi Apollinares | 212 BC | Apollo |
| July | 11 | Ludi victoriae Caesaris | 46 BC | Venus |
| September | 16 | Ludi Romani | Early | Jupiter |
| October | 7 | Ludi victoriae Sullanae | 82 BC | — |
| November | 14 | Ludi plebeii | 220 BC | Jupiter |

This totals seventy-seven days, and excluded from the total are the Quinquatrus, a festival of Minerva in March, and the Saturnalia (December), which were not *ludi*; occasional *ludi* (the Ludi Saeculares were celebrated every 100 or 110 years; at those held in 17 BC, a hymn written by Horace was performed by a choir of twenty-seven boys and twenty-seven girls); and festivals outside Rome, such as the Feriae Latinae, held on Mt Albanus. By about AD 354 the number had grown to 175 days in the year. We may perhaps compare the effect of the five-day week, which leads to 104, as against the original fifty-two non-working days a year, to which must be added bank holidays and two or three weeks' annual holiday. The earliest record of Christian observance of the Lord's Day comes from AD 202; and in AD 321 the emperor Constantine ordered that Sunday should be kept as a day free from all business, except for charitable acts like freeing a slave. In AD 416 we find the conservative pagan poet Rutilius Namatianus reacting to the work-free Sabbath with a satirical couplet which shows how alien this was to Roman tradition:

> *Each seventh day's condemned to sloth,*
> *To prove God lazy, weak, or both.*

The opening days of *ludi* were devoted to dramatic performances, the closing days to chariot racing. Plays could also be put on for other special occasions, eg Terence's comedy *Adelphoe* (160 BC), exhibited at the funeral games for Aemilius Paullus, and Varius' tragedy *Thyestes* (29 BC, not extant), presented at the triumphal games for the Battle of Actium. As in Greece, however, dramatic performances were not put on all the year round. For long there was no theatre in Rome, and performances were held in or near the particular shrines involved, where temporary wooden seating was erected. In fact strong prejudice was voiced by the senate against the construction of a permanent theatre, which evidently seemed to conservatives too Greek and corrupting an institution. In 155 BC work was started on a stone theatre, but the consul P. Scipio Nasica was successful in having it stopped. It was not until 100 years later that Rome's first stone theatre, Pompey's theatre, was built. It may have seated 9,000 or 10,000, not as the elder Pliny says 40,000, since the Forma Urbis Romae (ancient city plan) shows that it was too small for such a figure.

### THEATRES AND AMPHITHEATRES

A theatre and an amphitheatre had quite different shapes. Whereas the amphitheatre was elliptical, the Roman theatre was semicircular (p 52). This is a departure from the Greek theatre, which was contained in an arc somewhat greater than 180°. Unlike the Greek theatre, the Roman came increasingly to be built on masonry substructures and relied less on hill slopes. The wings of the stage had vaulted roofs, and there were doorways at various heights in the auditorium. The name *vomitoria*, attached by modern writers to one or both of these, has slender authority. It occurs only in Macrobius as an entrance for spectators at shows. A staircase linked the long stage to the orchestra, and the building was made an architectural whole, contrary to Greek practice, by fully linking auditorium and stage-building with walls. The seating occupied curved blocks, often rising to a considerable height. Whereas the Greek theatre had either no curtain or only a small one, the Roman theatre had a large curtain which was raised from the ground when ours is lowered from above and vice versa. It was made of canvas, evidently held up by some sort of pulley, and wound down into a recess below the stage. Virgil (*Georgics* iii. 24) refers to bright theatre curtains embroidered with figures of Britons.

The orchestra, which had been a dancing-place for the chorus in the Greek theatre, was reserved for senators in the theatre at Rome, in which no chorus performed. By a law of 67 BC, reinforcing an earlier law which had fallen into disuse, the first fourteen rows of the auditorium were reserved for knights (*equites*), who would thus be behind the senators but in front of the plebs. This measure, as can be expected, caused much dissatisfaction.

Under the Republic not only citizens but their wives, children and even (though not legally entitled) slaves were permitted to sit in any part of the auditorium allotted to the plebs. Foreigners, unless they were VIPs, had no right to attend. Augustus introduced segregation in the theatre, with separate blocks for women, slaves, and sons of *nobiles* with their *paedagogi*. Entrance tickets which have been discovered are marked with seat blocks but not with amounts of money, which may mean that admission was free.

## DRAMATIC PERFORMANCES

Tragedies and comedies were performed in the theatre at *ludi*. Early Roman tragedy was mainly based on Greek tragedies of the fifth century BC, and to judge from its fragments was clumsy in comparison with the originals. A complaint by Horace is that the Romans were too fond of grandiose shows, somewhat in the old lavish style of Hollywood's heyday, so that the action was held up while processions of horses and chariots filed past. Romans also had an unhealthy appetite for the most lurid of Greek plots, such as the myth of Thyestes of Mycenae, who at a banquet served up to his brother the flesh of that brother's own children. Horace, strongly critical, warned off the young playwright: 'Medea must not be allowed to slaughter her children in front of the audience.'

Early comedy was based on the Greek New Comedy of Menander (b 342–1 BC) and his contemporaries. It is clear from a Greek fragment discovered a few years ago that the *Bacchides* of Plautus, and therefore presumably his other plays, were adaptations of the Greek rather than faithful translations. Terence, who adapted six plays of the New Comedy, devotes his prologues to answering criticism (his audiences evidently wanted genuine Greek plays in translation) and encouraging his audience to attend patiently. Like all audiences in ancient theatres, they were seated out of doors. So one of his complaints is that they were too easily distracted by rival entertainments nearby, such as boxing, tight-rope walking and gladiatorial shows.

Rarer than adaptations of Greek tragedy and comedy were plays on purely Roman themes. Some of these were written about heroes of the past, such as Romulus or L. Junius Brutus, who expelled the Tarquins. It is disappointing that the only such play to survive entire, the *Octavia*, seems, as do the tragedies of Seneca, to have been written for something like a play-reading group (assuming that some wealthy men promoted these) rather than for the live stage.

The plays were performed by male actors, mostly freedmen and slaves, and often of foreign birth. On various occasions from 115 BC onwards we hear of expulsions of actors; and they could be whipped by magistrates, so that it is not surprising that their social status was low. Nevertheless in Cicero's time and just before, the actor Q. Roscius Gallus, who was of free birth and was made a knight by Sulla, was regarded as an absolutely superb performer in comedy, and left an enormous fortune. Actors were trained and managed by a professional producer.

Masks were of the same type as those worn on the Greek stage, but there are contradictory reports about the periods when they were used and when they were not. During the late Greek period a high buskin (actor's boot) had been introduced for tragic actors, and this was retained. There were usually three doors facing the audience, as well as side doors. Thus in a comedy the arrangement was that most of the action took place outside the front doors of the main characters' houses. The fact that performances took place in the open air lent them a certain aspect of realism. The actors could, if they wanted to, reach one house from another by a 'back lane' invisible to the audience. It was a convention, arising from the theatre at Athens, that characters coming from the country appeared on the left of the audience, those from the town or harbour on the right; the harbour was indeed on the right of spectators in the theatre of Dionysus at Athens. Asides were frequent, and non-speaking characters could be used. Music for the more choral passages was provided by a slave playing on pipes. It will be seen that in several respects the performances were more akin to the Elizabethan theatre (which in many ways imitated classical usage) than to the theatre of today. But with the return to the apron stage we have come nearer to the architecture of the ancient theatre.

Two popular forms of dramatic entertainment were the mime and the pantomime. The mime was an impromptu performance without masks by one or more actors or actresses, based on scenes of everyday life, including love scenes. Stricter Romans deplored the licence which permitted mime actresses (*mimae*) to perform naked at the Floralia. The origin of pantomimes is ascribed to two Greek freedmen in the age of Augustus. A pantomime (Greek, 'imitator of everything') was a solo male performer who, wearing a variety of masks, took many parts; he could have a chorus to fill in his plot.

### CHARIOT-RACING

The entertainment other than tragedy and comedy which formed part of the *ludi* was chariot-racing. The setting for it was a stadium, in Rome the Circus Maximus. The popular enthusiasm for it was unbelievable, far greater than that for motor and motor-cycle racing today. Juvenal remarked that in his day the common people of Rome seemed to care about only two things, *panem et circenses*, 'bread and the chariot races'. These kept growing in popular interest, partly because of keen betting on the outcome. The usual races were with two-horse or four-horse chariots, which started in twelve 'prisons' (*carceres*), ie boxes, set in an arc of a circle. When the magistrate waved down the cloth he was holding up, slaves let down cords which operated a simultaneous release of the 'prison' gates. The charioteers dashed round the right of the central division, grazing the turning-post at the end, and made seven laps. Under the Empire something slightly comparable to the idea of supporters following the fortunes of favourite football teams emerged in the shape of 'colours'. Originally there were four, whites, greens, reds and blues, with four chariots to each, but the numbers of chariots gradually increased. By the late Empire the rivalry was between the blues and the greens. The intense feeling between these factions, coupled with popular indignation that a favourite charioteer had been imprisoned, led to riots and a terrible massacre in Thessalonica (Saloniki) in AD 390. The emperor Theodosius, to avenge the death of a general in the riots, invited the inhabitants to a chariot race and had all comers slaughtered by his soldiers. The great charioteers of Rome and other large cities received as much hero-worship as any footballer today and amassed enormous fortunes. Among those who took part in chariot-races were the emperors Commodus and Caracalla. On the whole it was a spectacular sport, and as with today's crowds the spectators' energy, which might have been better used in exercise, was released in violence and vandalism.

### FIGHTS AND SHOWS IN THE AMPHITHEATRE

Gladiatorial and 'mock hunting' games attracted such large audiences in Rome that under the Flavian emperors of the late first century AD the Colosseum was erected chiefly to provide for them. Gladiatorial games, although not part of the *ludi* under the Republic, were introduced as early as 264 BC, originally as funeral games. The fact that at Rome they, like the *ludi*, were organised and paid for by aediles meant that there was competition for the most lavish production. In 22 BC a senate decree attempted to limit the size and duration of gladiatorial shows, but this remained a dead letter. Between AD 177 and 180 the expenses allowed for each type of gladiatorial games were limited. On two occasions we hear of as many as 10,000 gladiators fighting, once under Augustus and once under Trajan; Trajan's games lasted nearly four months. Free men could become gladiators, but normally did so only if driven by debt or despair. The majority were slaves, often from Thrace, which was reputed to breed particularly fierce men. They were trained in strictly controlled gladiatorial schools, each school running a troupe (*familia*, literally 'household'). They were specialised in function, with the intention that opponents should always be different types of fighter. Thus the *retiarius* wielded a net and a trident, aiming at throwing the net over his human or animal opponent; the Thraex (Thracian) had a scimitar and shield; the *mirmillo* and the Samnite were more heavily armed, with helmet, sword and shield.

*Venationes*, 'mock hunts', was the name given to amphitheatre shows involving wild or sometimes domestic animals. In the early second century BC the importation of wild animals was forbidden, but this law was later annulled, and we hear of *venationes* from 186 BC. The following figures, based mainly on Suetonius' lives of the Caesars and relating to individual celebrations, show the increasing numbers and also the increasing violence.

| Date | Number of animals and type of entertainment |
|---|---|
| 93 BC | 100 lions put on show |
| 58 BC | 1 hippopotamus, 5 crocodiles put on show in water |
| 55 BC | 600 lions, 20 elephants fought against African dart-throwers |
| AD 80 | 5,000 wild and 4,000 domestic animals killed at opening of Colosseum |
| AD 108–9 | 11,000 animals killed; 10,000 gladiators fought |

In the more accessible areas demand outgrew supply, and the ecology was disturbed; the younger Pliny laments that there are practically no more panthers to be found in Bithynia.

The games involving animals may be subdivided into (1) the exhibition of wild animals, (2) animals of different types fighting each other, eg elephants versus bulls, (3) gladiators versus animals, (4) animals let loose on unarmed criminals, Christians etc. The programme started with the gladiators paying their respects to the emperor, if present, using the formula *morituri te salutamus*, 'we who are going to die greet you.' But the emperor could at any stage give the signal for the sparing of a life, if for example he was impressed by the heroic qualities of a gladiator.

The killing of wild animals in the amphitheatre was probably no more and no less cruel than the baiting and killing of bulls at Spanish bull-fights. But the execution of condemned persons in this way was undoubtedly cruel, in particular when these were chained and had no opportunity of defending themselves. The Christian writers protested strongly against the whole system. The philosopher Seneca disliked the gladiatorial games, but reserved his strongest protests for special lunch-time ones at which the slaughter was more indiscriminate than at those more regularly attended. He evidently got through to the man in the street: a Pompeii graffito mentions him by name, and it has been thought that this may be in his capacity as a protester. It seems possible that accumulation of protests eventually had some effect, since under the late Empire gladiators fighting wild animals were better armed and so in less danger.

Mock naval battles (*naumachiae*) were sometimes staged in

an amphitheatre, for which purpose the barriers round the audience were cemented and the central ellipse flooded. Alternatively, either these or mock sea-fights on a smaller scale could be performed on a natural or artificial lake or pond: Horace addresses the sons of a noble family which from time to time put on such a show. The following are some well-known examples of the larger type, which were only occasional features.

| Date | Promoter | Place of performance | Total numbers | Supposed opponents |
|---|---|---|---|---|
| 46 BC | Julius Caesar | Rome | — | Tyrians, Egyptians |
| 2 BC | Augustus | Rome | 3,000 marines | Athenians, Persians |
| AD 52 | Claudius | Fucine Lake | 19,000 men; 24 or 50 ships | Sicilians, Rhodians |
| AD 80 | Titus | Rome | 3,000 marines | Athenians, Syracusans |

## OTHER SPORT

Too much of their sport was non-participatory. Personal physical exercise and sports never played the same part in the Roman as in the Greek world, and Romans were at times contemptuous of the endless hours of training put in by Greeks in the gymnasium or wrestling-school. The majority of the Greek forms of exercise, such as running, jumping, throwing the discus and the javelin, boxing, wrestling and ball games, were introduced into Rome in the second century BC. A Roman development in boxing was the introduction of the *caestus*, a glove weighted with iron and reinforced with metal spikes. This must have resulted in further brutalisation. Ball games were popular: Trimalchio, satirised in Petronius as a wealthy freedman who had come to Italy as a slave, insists, in his middle age, on a daily ball game. Swimming near Rome was mostly in the Tiber, opposite the Campus Martius and so above pollution level at the outflow of the Cloaca Maxima. Sunbathing and, under the

Empire, swimming in open-air pools came to be popular; the younger Pliny had a heated pool at his Laurentine villa. Swimming in the sea is occasionally mentioned; but from the great shortage of references it can hardly have been a very common pursuit. Romans visited seaside resorts for relaxation or convalescence, and for a change of climate from the heat of summer in Rome. Baiae on the Gulf of Naples was the most fashionable resort, while Tarentum was said to have the mildest climate in Italy.

### TOURIST ACTIVITIES

Tourism abroad was regarded as desirable extended education, mainly in the form of finding out about the antiquities of older civilisations. Students saw many of the monuments surviving from classical Greece when they visited Athens, Rhodes, Pergamum and other centres of learning. Other tourists assiduously visited many of the Greek tourist centres popular today, especially Athens, Delphi, Epidaurus and Olympia. Pausanias' guide to Greece, written in the second century AD, is as thorough as any Baedeker and still a good companion. The seven wonders of the ancient world were the pyramids; Phidias' gold and ivory statue of Zeus at Olympia; the Colossus of Rhodes (which had fallen in an earthquake in the third century BC); the Mausoleum, tomb of Mausolus, satrap of Caria; the hanging gardens of Babylon; the temple of Artemis at Ephesus; and the Pharos lighthouse at Alexandria (or the walls of Babylon).

Travel by sea, except in winter, was much faster than travel by land, so that, for tourism too, sea journeys of greater length became popular. Egypt was the main country concerned, and Romans were particularly impressed by the pyramids. One admirer of their architecture was the wealthy C. Cestius Epulo, who died before 12 BC and whose pyramidal tomb, quite different from that of most Romans, may be seen in Rome near the Porta S. Paolo. Another favourite object of sightseeing was the colossal statue at Thebes (near Luxor) said to be that of

Memnon but in reality that of Amenophis III. From time to time this statue gave off a resounding note, owing to rapidly changing temperatures, and visitors waited for this to happen, many of them recording their visits. Greek and/or Latin inscriptions on the statue total 109, dating from AD 20 to about AD 200; one is given in Chapter 9.

Yachting was a hobby for the rich: Catullus was fortunate to be able to buy a new yacht in Bithynia and take it all the way (including a short distance by land) to his native Lake Benacus (Garda). Hunting was a favourite countryside occupation, especially in autumn and winter. Deer and wild boar were the animals most generally hunted in Italy, while for big game the remoter parts of Asia Minor were the usual hunting-ground. By one procedure the huntsman on horseback, armed with hunting-spears, was accompanied by Molossian hounds, trained not to bark on seeing their quarry; by another the game was driven into nets. The younger Pliny, who found chariot-racing a bore, rather enjoyed hunting, but cannot have been very effective when he tried to combine lying in ambush with literary composition.

Two forms of competition mentioned by Virgil are a race by large oar-propelled boats and the *lusus Troiae* (taken by him to mean 'game of Troy', but probably meaning 'labyrinthine game'). This was a sort of equestrian labyrinthine manoeuvre and mock battle, performed by teams of twelve boys on horseback. Romans drove chariots on public roads, and the young were given to speed; but Juvenal thinks it very undignified when a consul has a craving for driving his own chariot and, being ashamed to drive it by day, exercises his hobby by night. Country walking and mountaineering were undertaken only as necessity demanded, and the emperor Hadrian was even thought eccentric for his love of walking to the tops of mountains to watch the sunrise.

## EVENING ENTERTAINMENT AND INDOOR GAMES

Of indoor games by far the commonest was dice-playing, with dice closely resembling ours. It was among other things one of the main forms of gambling, and there were professionals and special names for throws, eg Venus = three sixes. The emperor Claudius was so addicted to dice-playing that Seneca, in a skit on his deification, imagined him banished from heaven to Hades doomed to shake dice for ever in a bottomless dice-box. Figure 11 illustrates a typical game. The clean-shaven player is saying EXSI, ie probably *exii*, 'I've won' (see V. Väänänen, *Le latin vulgaire des inscriptions pompéiennes*, 3rd ed, p 112). The bearded player denies this by disputing the throw: 'It's not a three, it's a two.'

The game *duodecim scripta* (12 inscribed spaces) was played on a marked board actually containing twenty-four (2 × 12) squares, with fifteen white and fifteen black pieces. It was somewhat similar to backgammon, though three dice were used instead of two, and the white and black pieces started on one square each. *Latrunculi* (little robbers) was a complicated game with a large number of pieces. Contrary to what is sometimes stated, neither of these games was a form of chess.

Owing to difficulties of lighting, evening entertainment was far more restricted than today. Music and dancing did not occupy the same position in Roman life as in Greek; they tended to be left to professionals. 'Practically no one who is sober', wrote Cicero, 'dances, unless he happens to be mad.' Musicians or singers were sometimes brought in to entertain guests at a dinner-party. Seneca disapproved of the rowdy musical beach parties typical of the Naples area. One of the minor poems attributed to Virgil is addressed to a Syrian girl who at a country restaurant in Italy, perhaps inland from Naples, welcomed passing travellers and sang and performed sinuous dances, which may have been somewhat akin to the belly-dancers' displays in the Arab world. When Horace mentions the greasy cookhouse as one of the attractions of Rome for the countryman, he couples with it the brothel. Prostitutes were usually slaves, sometimes Greek-speaking girls of great accom-

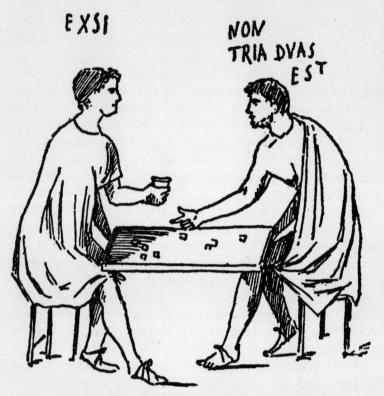

Fig 11    Two dice-players, from a Pompeii fresco

plishments. There were many restaurants on the main roads in Italy: one stopping-place on the Via Appia acquired the name Tres Tabernae, 'three taverns'. In the large towns were what would be called inns rather than hotels, providing board, lodging and stabling. Figure 12 illustrates a typical scene, in which four men, two of whom are travellers wearing capes, are seated on benches at a table. Travellers constantly complained of cheating, overcharging, noise and insolent behaviour by ostlers and other servants. Cicero avoided inns to a large extent by buying up and maintaining a whole chain of villas on or near the coast south of Rome. He used some of these also for summer relaxation, and invited guests to dinner parties.

Fig 12    Tavern scene, from a Pompeii fresco

### ARMY LEISURE

The army personnel occupied its leisure time in very much the same way as civilians. The soldier, like the civilian, took a midday siesta when conditions permitted, and permanent camps were equipped with good bath buildings. Wherever the legionaries went they imported their home activities. Thus a town like Caerleon needed a large amphitheatre because of the number of soldiers stationed there. Leave was granted to soldiers under the late Republic and Empire on payment of a fee to their centurions. It was regarded as a comparative hardship to be posted to somewhere like Hadrian's Wall, where leisure opportunities were more restricted than in a luxurious province such as Syria. It is perhaps unexpected that even the composition of poetry was not neglected in certain army units. Thus Augustus' stepson the future emperor Tiberius, when he led a semimilitary, semi-diplomatic mission to the East in 20 BC to negotiate for the return of Roman legionary standards from the Parthians, took with him a retinue of young nobles, most of whom had some literary interest. We also hear of Cicero's brother Quintus adapting Greek plays while he was on Julius Caesar's staff in Gaul.

### WOMEN'S LEISURE OCCUPATIONS

Married women, especially of the wealthier classes, were enabled by the system of slavery to devote a good proportion of their time to leisure pursuits. These included reading, writing poetry or listening to it, painting, embroidery, and playing musical instruments or listening to music. They also attended theatrical performances (see p 146 for seats allocated to them), chariot races and gladiatorial games. They went to the baths, and also spent leisure time shopping, but the variety of goods for sale other than in food shops would be considered poor by modern standards. Of domestic pets, dogs and cage-birds were the commonest. Lesbia's *passer* whose death Catullus lamented is thought to have been a rock thrush (*Monticola solitarius*), which has an attractive blue colouring. Parrots were imported from the East at great cost, and Statius has an obituary poem on one of these, which he calls 'leader of birds'. Cats were popular in Egypt but not in Rome.

Children too played with pet dogs and birds. But they also had toys such as terracotta dolls, rattles, balls, hoops and tops. Miniature furniture was used both as toys and for votive offerings. Among games played more by children than adults were knuckle-bones, coin tossing and a game still played in Italy in which two people shoot out fingers simultaneously and try to guess how many.

### THE BATHS

A pleasure not yet described is that of going to the public baths. Those who had no facilities at home regularly went almost as a necessity, a wealthier man being accompanied by a slave to carry his towel, scraper and other things. But in one way the baths had something of the atmosphere of a café, where one could indulge in gossip or transact business. *Thermae* (hot baths) was the name for the larger and better equipped establishments, *balnea* or *balneae* for smaller baths. In many of the larger baths there were separate facilities for men and women; the water was usually heated from the same furnaces. The commonest time for men to take a bath was the eighth hour in summer, the ninth in winter; these work out at a roughly similar time of day, 2.15 or 2.30 pm. In smaller baths separate hours could be prescribed for the two sexes. Thus at the Vipasca mining settlement in Spain the costs and hours were:

Men $\frac{1}{2}$ as Eighth hour to second hour of the night
Women 1 as Morning and early afternoon up to seventh hour

In Rome of classical times the costs were half these amounts; we hear also of free baths financed by legacies. Mixed bathing is disapproved of by the elder Pliny and had several times to be forbidden by law. The order of using rooms in the baths was: (1) *tepidarium*, for immersion in warm water; (2) *caldarium*, hot bath, after which one was oiled with olive oil and rubbed down with a scraper (*strigil*); (3) *frigidarium*, cold bath; (4) *caldarium* again, if required. From about 100 BC hypocausts were used for heating the baths. The architecture was designed so that the hottest rooms were nearest to the furnace. The noise coming from the public baths, we are told by Seneca, was terrific; he had lodgings over them (*Epistles* lvi. 1–2), and heard men exercising with dumb-bells, masseurs, a ball-boy, a bully, a thief caught in the act, a man who loved singing in the bath, men who liked splashing into the water, and the sellers of cakes, sausages and other foods shouting out their wares.

## LITERARY PURSUITS

Literary pursuits as leisure activities were fashionable, perhaps akin to the salons of France or the coffee-houses of eighteenth-century England. A relatively large number of Romans, including emperors and a few women, developed the habit of writing poems in their spare time. 'We all,' says Horace, 'educated and uneducated, write poems everywhere.' Some time in the first century BC the habit grew up of inviting friends or dependants (*clientes*) to hear the reading of a poem or part of one, or more rarely a piece of prose. Since there was nothing like a literary review, this served as a useful means of introducing a forthcoming work to the reading public. Virgil introduced some of his poetry to Augustus and the imperial family by such preliminary readings, and we are told by Donatus that when the poet reached the famous passage in which he described Marcellus, Augustus' nephew and intended heir who had just died (23 BC), Octavia the bereaved mother fainted. Horace was afraid that this love of poetry readings (*recitationes*) would, as happened later, result in 'playing to the gods'. He wrote: 'I don't read my poetry to anyone except friends, and then only when I'm forced to.' The younger Pliny in a letter complains that during the whole of one April there was hardly a day in Rome when someone was not holding a literary session. Tacitus describes the poor conditions under which certain of these poetry readings were held, in a rickety hall hired from a nobleman at great cost, to which was added the cost of hiring chairs. Juvenal satirises the institution by complaining: 'Am I never to retaliate after so often putting up with an epic on Theseus by the hoarse poet Codrus?' The reading was not always done by the author himself. Claudius, before he became emperor, had written antiquarian works on the Etruscans and the Carthaginians. When he unwillingly succeeded to the principate he realised he was in a stronger position to command an audience, so gave instructions that these works of his were to be read out at intervals in public libraries. Reading at home for pleasure was common; most ancients read aloud.

Ever since the great Greek library in Alexandria had been founded by Ptolemy Soter (King of Egypt 304–283 or 282 BC), the need for libraries in large cities had become apparent. Yet Rome had to wait for a public library until C. Asinius Pollio, from the spoils received from his Illyrian victory in 39 BC, built the first one. Augustus founded two, one on the Palatine and one on the Campus Martius. Each had a Greek section, a Latin section, a foyer in which readers could meet and converse, and an adjacent temple. The libraries were adorned with statues of great writers of the past. Other emperors followed this lead, and eventually there were twenty-six or twenty-nine in Rome. Elsewhere too there were public libraries erected either by emperors or private citizens; thus the younger Pliny paid for one to be founded at his native Comum (Como), and Hadrian had a fine one built in Athens. At Tibur (Tivoli), books could be borrowed as well as read on the spot.

Many of the wealthier Romans had extensive libraries of their own. Under the late Republic Lucullus and Cicero had some of the largest collections. The largest private collection recorded under the Empire is of 30,000 volumes. The most famous discovered was the library of a large villa at Herculaneum explored in 1752. About 1,800 papyrus rolls and fragments were discovered, charred by lava from the eruption of Vesuvius, and it proved very difficult to unwind them. When, at the beginning of the nineteenth century, a number were deciphered, they turned out to be works of the Greek philosopher Philodemus. It is almost certain that the villa belonged in the late Republic to L. Calpurnius Piso, Philodemus' patron, and later to his heirs.

A typical literary collector of the late first century AD was the poet Silius Italicus (AD 26–101). After a lifetime of public service (some of it not above suspicion, because he was thought to have given false evidence as an informer), he settled down in his villa near the Gulf of Naples to write an indifferent historical epic in seventeen books on the Second Punic War. He was such a keen admirer of Virgil that he imitated his works, collected anything connected with him and revered and repaired his tomb. Fortunately, in spite of barbarian invasions, the habit of book collecting received a fresh impetus in the fourth and fifth centuries AD, when classical poets began to be studied again with enthusiasm, and when Claudian, Ausonius and others wrote poetry inspired by Virgil and his successors (p 166). In the mid sixth century AD we find Cassiodorus, after a busy political life, setting up a learned religious community called Vivarium in Calabria and retiring there with a large library. In ways like this, such private collections as escaped the ravages of invaders often found their way into monasteries and were copied out by the monks.

### ART AS A HOBBY

Romans did not regard painting as a leisure activity. But the collecting of works of art was one of the favoured pursuits of the richer Romans, the commonest being statuary. More marble statues than bronze have survived, because in the Dark Ages bronze was frequently melted down. Marble statues were often painted, and eyes could be represented by precious stones. We tend to think of ancient marbles as unpainted because the paint wears off, and because Renaissance imitations of ancient statuary were not painted over. Almost every notable house in Pompeii had statuary of one kind or another, especially imitations of Greek works. In 1957 a cave on the beach at Sperlonga (from Latin *spelunca* = cave) south of Terracina was discovered and excavated. It turned out to contain over 5,500 fragments of statuary. Certainly this was a special case, as it was associated with the emperor Tiberius, who had a villa there. Among the finds were some gigantic pieces, one originally 6m (20ft) high, which must have represented sea-serpents sent to punish the Trojan priest Laocoon and his sons who had argued against taking the wooden horse into Troy. It looks from an inscription as though the group was made by the three Rhodian sculptors of the first century BC mentioned by the elder Pliny as creators of the famous Laocoon group. The question arises whether the well-known Vatican group or the Sperlonga fragments, which seem to have been differently arranged, are the ones Pliny was talking about. It is perhaps typical of the Roman approach to statuary that he marvels chiefly at the construction of a Laocoon group all in one block. It was thought that the Vatican Laocoon was made in a single block, but it is now known not to have been.

## RETIREMENT

Retirement did not pose the leisure problems that it does today. The average age at death was much lower than in Western Europe now, according to most calculations forty to fifty, so that few had years of retirement to provide for. Moreover there was no fixed retirement age. True, sixty was the age at which men were excluded from the voting-pens, but it was never an age at which one had to retire from office. Senators remained members of the senate for life and were expected, if fit, to continue taking part in its deliberations. The only emperors who retired were Diocletian and Maximian, both perhaps in their mid sixties in AD 305. There are known cases of high office continued into old age: L. Calpurnius Piso was Prefect of the City of Rome from the age of sixty to his death at eighty (AD 32), and C. Turranius at eighty was allowed by the emperor Gaius to continue as Prefect of Corn Supply when he put on an act preparing for death on being superannuated. Civil servants too were not necessarily retired at a fixed age: Statius' friend the father of Claudius Etruscus came to Rome from Smyrna and served a succession of emperors, apart from a period of exile in old age, until he died in AD 92 at nearly ninety. Quintilian retired from his teaching appointment when he was about fifty-five, still vigorous but wanting time to write his book on the training of orators. Statius himself was probably under fifty when he moved from the area near Alba Longa to Naples. He still wrote poetry for a few years while suffering from insomnia, but no longer lived an active life and found that his intended *magnum opus*, an epic on the life of Achilles, was 'sticking'.

Legionaries normally retired at forty-six, but were then given holdings of land, so that most of them changed their occupation to farming or horticulture for the rest of their lives. Those with specialised training, such as military surveyors, were not uncommonly called up again in any emergency. Old retainers might be active or might hang around the houses of their masters or patrons doing little. Comedy, based on Greek tradition, portrayed old slaves of both sexes as wine-bibbers. Seneca, who was usually sympathetic to slaves, looked with repugnance on an old retainer, well-known to him in his younger days, who had become ugly and deformed and was squatting idly by the doorpost. But slaves were at least kept and fed, however long they lived: this was actually a legal requirement.

# 9

# *What Survives from the Roman World*

THE legacy of the Roman world may be assessed from three angles: (1) the written word; (2) the material remains, including objects of art; (3) the legacy of ideas.

## THE WRITTEN WORD

The whole of Western civilisation today has been built on Roman cultural foundations as strong as Rome's physical structures. In some aspects of its legacy there has been a continuous tradition ever since. This is particularly true of the survival of Latin literature. Texts were copied and re-copied on papyrus or parchment. A fair percentage probably lasted only a few years. But quotations by Latin grammarians of the fourth and fifth centuries AD and other writers show that much more was available to them than to us. The works we possess may mainly be divided into four categories: (1) works of special literary value; (2) school texts; (3) Christian works, which might well be copied irrespective of literary value; (4) reference or technical works. If, as is the case with Virgil's and Horace's poems, posterity judged them both as great literature and as good educational material, they were likely to survive complete. But literary critics under the late Empire had their own ideas of what constituted literature worth preserving; thus the *Annals* of Ennius (written about 190–180 BC) have not been pre-

served except in fragments, simply because they were then held
to be archaic and inartistic, whereas the rather dull epic of Silius
Italicus (pp 161–2) has survived in its entirety, possibly because
he was regarded as an historical authority. Yet both works dealt
with the same great war won by Rome, of which Ennius had
actually been an eye-witness.

Our earliest surviving Latin literary manuscripts, apart from
fragments, date from the fourth and fifth centuries AD. They
include one manuscript of Terence's comedies and several of
Virgil, with illustrations whose colour is well preserved. Of
prose authors, we have a palimpsest (twice-used manuscript) of
Cicero's *Republic* which dates from the fourth century, while
manuscripts of other writers are later; in fact the preservation
of the *Annals* of Tacitus, one of the most outstanding histories of
all time, rests on a slender thread, Books I–VI being unknown
to the scholarly world before the sixteenth century.

The revival of learning which occurred in the fourth and fifth
centuries AD had its origin in an educational impetus in some of
the outlying parts of the Roman Empire. The foundation of
Constantinople in AD 330 led to a fusion of Greek and Roman
educational systems which had the effect of encouraging learning. Papyrus finds from Egypt show that Latin poetry came to
be studied more there at this period. Claudian, the last good
Latin poet, who wrote in Italy between AD 395 and 405, was
educated in Alexandria; the great Christian writer Augustine,
educated in North Africa, taught rhetoric both there and in
Rome and Milan; the poet and rhetorician Ausonius was
educated at Bordeaux and Toulouse: all of these were famous
centres of learning. In Constantinople fifteen professors of Greek
and thirteen of Latin were endowed by the state in 425. In
Italy itself literature continued well after the fall of Rome: one
of the more prolific prose writers was Cassiodorus (c 490–c 583),
an important minister under King Theodoric; he tried without
success to found a Christian university at Rome.

From the sixth, seventh and eighth centuries the Latin
manuscripts handed down to us are more Christian than pagan.
But there was a revival of the copying of classical Latin texts

under Charlemagne, who ordered that monks should brush up their Latin grammar for this purpose. From the ninth to the fifteenth centuries we have a continuous series of manuscripts, copied out in the Middle Ages by monks and in the Renaissance (literally 're-birth', ie of classical ideas) by scholars or their copyists. In the early fifteenth century came a wave of new discoveries: Renaissance scholars like Poggio visited monasteries and searched their libraries for hitherto unknown works. Already in the Middle Ages much influence of Latin poetry, especially Virgil, Ovid, Lucan and Statius, on European literature is to be seen. In the Renaissance this is supplemented by the influence of the fourth category listed above, technical writing. Thus, study of Vitruvius' work on architecture had as its application a profound effect on the architecture of Renaissance Italy. Even so, the full technical details to be found in Vitruvius were not understood at the time, eg his explanation of heating systems. Europeans might have advanced more rapidly towards living conditions typical of the nineteenth and twentieth centuries if at any time scholars had been more interested in technical writings.

In the Middle Ages the monks had preserved and recopied many manuscripts of books. Practically none, however, took the trouble to preserve such items as legal documents, lists of magistrates, records of triumphs or laudatory epitaphs, some of which were carved on stone, as being intended for lasting record, while others were recorded on much more perishable materials like papyrus. Records written on wax tablets decayed, those on bronze tablets (including for example the plans and maps of the land surveyors) were melted down. The only Roman map of the known world which has come down to us with the slightest resemblance to what may have been its original is the very elongated Peutinger Table. Yet the Forma Urbis Romae, a marble plan of Rome dating from soon after AD 200, has survived in substantial fragments. Inscriptions were mostly on stone; enormous numbers have been preserved in whole or in part, and many more may yet be revealed through excavation.

One of the most interesting inscriptions is Augustus' *Res Gestae* (Achievements), preserved partly in Latin and partly in Greek. It was published immediately after his death in multiple copies distributed through the provinces to be carved in stone and set up in public places. We can ignore its tone of propaganda and its intentional omissions, and can learn much from its factual information, wishing that there were even more figures than there are. Another of the more useful inscriptions gives us the charter of the mining settlement at Urso (Osuna) in southern Spain, issued by Mark Antony on behalf of Julius Caesar. An inscription discovered at Lyons in 1528 records the speech of the emperor Claudius on the admission of Gallic chieftains to membership of the Senate, so that it is possible to make a rare and fascinating comparison of the effects of different media. The inscribed stone gives the exact words of the emperor, pedantic in its antiquarian detail, verbose and full of digressions, whereas in Tacitus (*Annals* xi. 24) is a historian's précis of the same speech, an impressionistic and artistic version.

The following are three specimens of inscription in translation; such inscriptions help in the detective work of reconstructing Roman civilisation.

(1)  *16 March*   *Tiberius Caesar died at Misenum.*
    *30 March*   *His body brought to Rome by soldiers.*
    *3 April*   *Public funeral for the emperor.*
    *1 May*   *Antonia mother of Claudius died.*
    *1 June*   *Public distribution of money, 75 denarii a head.*
    *19 July*   *Second public distribution of 75 denarii a head.*

Extract from Fasti of Ostia for AD 37. The accession of the emperor Gaius (Caligula) is not mentioned, although his three-month consulship is given, as records of his reign were ordered after his death to be deleted.

(2) *I, Funisulana Vettulla, wife of C. Tettius Africanus, Prefect of Egypt, heard Memnon on 12 February, at 1½ hours, in the first year of Domitian's principate, this being my third visit.*

Inscription of AD 82 on the 'statue of Memnon' mentioned in Chapter 8.

> (3) *If modesty in life is thought*
> *To be of some avail,*
> *Then every honour surely ought*
> *To go to Lucretius Fronto.*

This inscription was painted on the street near the house of Lucretius Fronto in Pompeii. The English doggerel attempts to reproduce the effect of the Latin verse, in which the name Lucretius Fronto has been substituted for another name.

## THE MATERIAL REMAINS

Roman public buildings were essentially solidly built. By means of a much greater use of the arch and the vault and by facing brick with marble and/or incorporating concrete, they were able to construct larger and more permanent buildings than anyone succeeded in doing for centuries after the fall of the Roman Empire. Their state of preservation today varies considerably. In Rome and nearer parts of the Empire, there were so many large and monumental public buildings that instead of being destroyed in the Dark Ages a good proportion were used for other purposes. Those best preserved include a number of basilicas (public halls) adapted for use as Christian churches: they were repaired at regular intervals.

Among temples of interest are (1) circular: Rome, Temple of Vesta, and Pantheon (built by Hadrian on the site of Agrippa's temple in honour of all the gods; this had been destroyed in AD 80 and its successor in 110); (2) rectangular: Nîmes, Maison Carrée, originally dedicated to Rome and Augustus, subsequently to Augustus' grandsons; Pula, temple of Augustus. Of the three orders of architecture used in Greek temples, the Doric fell into disuse, the Ionic continued to be popular, while the Corinthian was modified slightly to give a distinctive Roman Corinthian capital.

Private houses, less solidly constructed, have disappeared on the surface in Rome, though many later buildings obviously used their foundations. They can most extensively be investigated at the city of Pompeii, long covered by volcanic ash, and at the ruins of Rome's harbour town, Ostia; though even at an outpost like Vindolanda, just south of Hadrian's Wall, foundations of housing of a surprisingly high standard have emerged on excavation. The centre of Ostia has been fully excavated, and its houses and shops are in most areas preserved to a height of 2–3m (6–10ft), in some cases higher. One of the best preserved has a niche, near the entrance, for a *lararium*, shrine to the *lares*, gods of the hearth.

One of a number of towns, and perhaps the most fascinating, in which Roman buildings have survived is Aosta, founded by Augustus as a colony under the title of Augusta Praetoria. It gives a good opportunity of comparing the ancient with the modern town plan. One may assume that its remote position, below the difficult St Bernard passes, assisted the preservation of features such as the triumphal arch of 24 BC, erected after A. Terentius Varro Murena had defeated the Alpine tribe Salassi; the theatre, with massive stage-buildings; the walls and gates, and several towers. But most striking of all are the Roman guardrooms still occupied, now, by shops and living accommodation, including even an *albergo*. Since the construction of the tunnels under the Alps, Aosta has been rapidly expanding. The old town has changed little, and the alignment and width of the streets bear a close resemblance to their ancient counterparts; but the traffic is now directed round the arch instead of under it as it was right up to the opening of the tunnel, and old decrepit buildings are being taken down so as to expose more Roman foundations.

A prominent feature of many Roman cities is the amphitheatre, and a number of these are in good state of preservation. The Colosseum (originally Flavian amphitheatre) in Rome provided a pattern for others. One of the best preserved is at

El Djem (ancient Thysdrus), Tunisia. In Arles in southern France and several Spanish cities the amphitheatre is used for bull-fights today. At Pula, ancient Pola, on the Istrian peninsula, the amphitheatre narrowly escaped in 1583 being transported stone by stone to Venice. Theatres too are preserved in several places, particularly well at Orange in southern France and the Graeco-Roman theatre at Aspendos in southern Turkey.

The services of Roman towns can also be studied from their remains. In addition to the numerous aqueducts of Rome, there are many in Italy and the provinces. The most architecturally pleasing is the Pont du Gard, near Nemausus (Nîmes), southern France. Among aqueducts still in use are those at Sulmo (Sulmona), central Italy, and at Segovia; the latter brings water to this Spanish city from the Rio Frio in the Sierra de Guadarrama, 16km (10 miles) away. Two of the most famous bridges are also in Spain, the long bridge at Augusta Emerita (Mérida), built under Augustus, and the high bridge at Alcántara, near the frontier with Portugal, erected in a joint effort by several communities in AD 106.

Even in Britain the attention paid to public services can be studied. An extensive sewerage system found under a building site between Church St and Swinegate, York, in 1972 (p 104) had clean and foul water efficiently separated in a way that could have taught civil engineers as late as the nineteenth century a few useful lessons. The drain was built about AD 200, and has been explored for about 50m (55yd). The roof is some 1m 50 (5ft) from the floor, and there are at intervals connecting sewers at right angles, leading to lavatories in the adjacent Roman houses. The most extensive urban site preserved in Britain is Verulamium, on the outskirts of St Albans, replanned on a large site by Agricola after its destruction.

Among the most solid buildings were the great imperial baths, symmetrical in design, with huge rooms vaulted in concrete. The best preserved specimens of these are the Baths of Caracalla and of Diocletian in Rome; the latter are used as a museum.

The remains of military camps are not as striking on the whole as those of civilian buildings, since some were purely temporary structures, while some were merged in the towns into which they grew. In this sphere Britain has much to offer, especially in Northumberland and Scotland, eg at Housesteads, at Inchtuthil, and on the Antonine Wall, where recent finds have been made at Bearsden, near Glasgow; there are also good specimens in various parts of Germany. Siege camps have been excavated in many places, notably Numantia, Spain, and Masada, Israel.

The remains of Roman villas may be studied in the countryside of Italy and in most of the provinces. In size and splendour they range from Hadrian's villa near Tibur (Tivoli), which aimed at including representative features from all the parts of the Empire that the emperor had visited, and which approached the size of a small town, to the very ordinary farm-house type. In Britain the earliest villas are of timber and stone, with slaves' quarters separate. Some of the most luxurious are as late as the fourth century AD. One of the largest villas in Britain is Chedworth in the Cotswolds, which had baths heated by hypocaust. Some farms had very large outbuildings. At the Bignor villa, Sussex, the livestock accommodation was large enough for the farm to store and use over 5,000 wagon-loads of farmyard manure a year.

Mosaics, because of their non-perishable materials, have been preserved all over the Roman Empire. On the floors of Roman villas in Britain they are a very common feature, either with plain geometrical designs or pictorial. Some of the finest pictorial ones are at the villa at Lullingstone, Kent. A late villa at Low Ham, Somerset, revealed mosaics with a number of illustrations from the *Aeneid*. Quite different in scale is the palace at Fishbourne, near Chichester, almost certainly the residence of the client king Ti. Claudius Cogidubnus. But the most superb must surely be some of those in North Africa and those in the villa or palace at Casale near Piazza Armerina in Sicily, dating from about AD 300.

Although excavation is constantly revealing new Roman

buildings, much is likely to escape observation. Modern towns are so often on Roman foundations that a large percentage is likely to remain buried. But discoveries are constantly being made, eg under St Peter's in Rome, York Minster and many other churches. Motorways take straightened routes, coping in their way with gradients, for the first time since the Roman occupation, and so may result in the destruction of Roman roads and sites alongside. Yet urban development, and the need to strengthen old foundations, can also be thanked for numerous discoveries of hitherto unknown sites. The Department of the Environment in Britain and government organisations in other countries are pouring money into short-term rescue operations, which are causing archaeologists to work faster than ever before. World War II bombing had earlier revealed important items such as the temple of Mithras in central London.

Some of the greatest possibilities for the future development of the discovery of Roman sites would seem to stem from aerial photography and underwater archaeology. The resources of aerial photography have already revealed detailed patterns of settlement, especially in Italy and France. In areas of the Roman Empire hitherto comparatively unknown from the point of view of settlement, such as Tunisia, they have shown field patterns and centuriation, the dividing up of land into squares mostly with sides 705–10m (771–7yd) long. Aerial photography in the African provinces has also shown where the boundary (*limes*) of the Roman Empire lay. But in other areas, eg in Spain and Turkey and off many of the Mediterranean coasts, much remains to be done. By means of underwater archaeology it may be possible to plot and find further remains of towns like Baiae, on the Gulf of Naples, of which over half has disappeared beneath the sea owing to earth movements (the whole area is still very liable to earthquakes as evidenced by the Pozzuoli movements of 1971). Such archaeology can now go hand in hand with research which is attempting to record the line of the coast at various points on the Mediterranean at different periods.

ART FINDS

Objects of art found are innumerable. Sculpture consisting of copies of Greek works, a feature common in Roman public and private buildings, is most informative when the Greek original has not survived; if there are several Roman copies, some idea can be obtained of the exact appearance of the original. In the case of Roman portrait statuary, the appearance of famous men can be traced over their careers with the help of coins and, under the late Empire, of medallions and consular diptychs; but Renaissance representations of ancient Romans must usually be considered wholly unrealistic. More detailed research can be attempted on the hair styles of men and women. Men's hair styles changed often; in Augustus' time one style was to have two partings. In the Flavian period some ladies of fashion wore high, curled wigs, while others had artificial waves with a central parting. Beards come and go: they were out of fashion from the time of the early Republic, returned to popularity under Hadrian, but tended to disappear from the third century AD onwards.

Painting is best preserved in the Pompeii frescoes, as described in Chapter 5. Studies of architectural vistas in these frescoes have thrown light on the interesting problems of perspective in ancient painting. A series of paintings in the Vatican Museum on the wanderings of Ulysses is perhaps the most absorbing of mythological subjects. It is clearly based on a lost Greek original, but we have no other Roman copy with which to compare it. The student of Roman painting can be helped (1) by verbal descriptions, eg those in the elder Pliny or in the Greek writer Philostratus; (2) by comparison with mosaics; (3) for the later period, by comparison with the art of the manuscript miniature.

A fair amount of Roman silver has been preserved. Among the best specimens of the early Empire is a collection of tableware from Boscoreale, near Vesuvius, with hunting and other scenes embossed. All the villas round the volcano were, like Pompeii and Herculaneum, destroyed by the eruption of AD 79; this collection seems to have been temporarily deposited in an agricultural factory. The Hildesheim treasure, found in south Hanover, is thought to date from the age of Augustus, and may have come from the camp of P. Quinctilius Varus, ambushed in the Teutoburg Forest in AD 9; there is a large mixing-bowl with floral relief, and drinking-bowls with mythological subjects. British enthusiasts are fortunate in being able to study the Mildenhall hoard in the British Museum. It was discovered at Mildenhall, Suffolk, by a ploughman during World War II. It consists of some thirty-two pieces, and although it dates from the later Empire (fourth century AD), the workmanship is particularly fine. The largest piece is a dish 60cm (2ft) in diameter, whose centre features a mask of Oceanus, and which has two borders, one of Nereids and sea monsters, one of a Bacchic procession. The British Museum also has some very fine pieces of the Esquiline Treasure, including two silver caskets, one of which was a wedding present to the Christian lady Projecta. It bears the inscription SECVNDE ET PROIECTA VIVATIS IN CHRISTO, 'Secundus and Projecta, may you live in Christ'.

Gold and precious stones are less commonly preserved, though it is clear from ancient sources that they were owned in abundance by the wealthy. The Archaeological Museum in Naples has many gold ornaments from Pompeii and Herculaneum, especially bracelets, rings, earrings, necklaces and *bullae* (amulets worn by young nobles). Rings were made of gold, silver, bronze, iron, glass or jet; some contained precious or semi-precious stones. Brooches (*fibulae*) were needed for fastening clothes, but ornamental ones in bronze or other metals are common.

Glass has been found widely, as it was generally used both for windows and skylights, and for drinking vessels, perfume bottles etc; the latter are often found in tombs. It is now often slightly opaque and of greenish colour, depending on the conditions under which it has been preserved.

Pottery was so mass-produced that it lacks the fine touch of Greek work. The commonest type is Terra Sigillata, which has a red gloss-coat. This Arretine ware is found both plain and moulded with reliefs. In the first century AD the plain ware was imitated in Asia Minor and, according to the elder Pliny, in the island of Samos. The decorative ware found in Britain and known as samian ware is not, however, connected with Samos, but with Gaul. The ornamentation is drawn mainly from classical mythology. Many of the vessels are stamped with potters' names. Since these can be given sequence dates by comparing the strata in which they were excavated, a whole chronological system is able to be built up, which may be of enormous value for the interpretation of new excavations.

Earthenware was used for large wine and oil vessels, tiles and guttering. Underwater archaeology has resulted in the discovery of large quantities of *amphorae* from wrecked ships off the coasts of the Mediterranean. From finds of wine and oil vessels on farms it is sometimes possible to estimate the annual production of the estates.

### MISCELLANEOUS FINDS

Remains of arms and armour have been found on many battle sites, as also trappings for horses, chariot wheels (most of a chariot was made of wood, so rarely survives), legionary standards, and documents such as tablets of honourable discharge. The camp at Inchtuthil, Perthshire, yielded enormous numbers of iron nails.

Commercial and technical finds include, in addition to accounts and medical prescriptions (mainly in Greek on papyri from Egypt), such items as surgical instruments and architects', surveyors', carpenters' and blacksmiths' tools. In the areas devastated by Vesuvius the buildings themselves have left clues to the trades exercised in them, while elsewhere we often have to turn to such evidence as tombstones, some of which have only inscriptions, while others have representations of artisans' tools. Pompeii and Herculaneum were so suddenly obliterated by the eruption that they have preserved evidence of technology better than other sites. Thus the only surveyor's workshop, complete with the instruments of his profession, was excavated at Pompeii in 1912. The town was not a great manufacturing centre, though it did produce among other things wine, fish sauce and perfumes. Here and elsewhere pottery kilns and bakery ovens may be seen, and there are remains of smithies, glassworks, tile manufacture and shops of various kinds with their equipment. A certain number of water-wheels and other milling equipment have survived. From the wine and oil trades a few presses are preserved (reconstructions can be seen to good advantage in the museum at Pula, Yugoslavia), as well as the numerous *amphorae* and other large earthenware containers.

Relatively few gold or silver coins have been preserved, but a great many bronze and copper. Coins are helpful in establishing dates and names, and are also revealing from the point of view of propaganda. New wording on coins occurred more frequently than on modern coins, almost rivalling today's issues of postage stamps. Thus in 20 BC when Augustus felt that his bargain with the Parthians, retrieving the standards lost by Crassus at the battle of Carrhae (53 BC), could be turned to good account, he issued coins with the inscription SIGNIS RECEPTIS, 'return of the standards'. Abstract nouns were much used with an emperor's name as a more general form of propaganda, eg PROVIDENTIA AVGVSTORVM, 'the foresight of the Augusti' (coin issued by Gordian II, AD 238). Even under the Republic, when coins were issued by monetary commissioners for the most part, we encounter occasional propaganda: for example, M. Brutus, in the last violent stages, issued a coin whose reverse shows the cap of liberty between two daggers, and the inscription EID.MAR. (Ides of March), to celebrate the assassination of Julius Caesar in 44 BC.

THE LEGACY OF IDEAS AND
CONTINUITY OF TRADITION

There is much more, however, to Roman civilisation than its visible remains. The original excitement in the Renaissance arose from the discovery of new manuscripts, together with horror at the rate at which the remains of ancient Rome were disappearing. But soon came the realisation that the legacy of Greece and Rome consists among other things of literary, philosophical, historical and artistic tradition. Rome absorbed the culture of Greece, and Western Europe has absorbed both as passed on by the Roman Empire. Latin drama took over the conventions of Greek tragedy and comedy, making the terminology more precise by talking about the acts of a play where Greek plays had had only dialogue divided by choral interludes. Horace proclaims:

> *A play that aims to be a great success*
> *Should have five acts—just five, no more, no less.*

This, coming from the pen of one who was the equivalent of poet laureate, was generally taken as authoritative for all time. Hence French classical tragedy and Elizabethan plays do have five acts.

The West European national languages, as they developed, retained the literary forms of Greek and Latin literature. In the Middle Ages any poet worthy of his calling would read and absorb Virgil's *Aeneid* and other major works of the classical period. The philosophers' sources were Aristotle's works in Latin translation, Cicero and Seneca. For rhetorical theory Cicero and Quintilian were the guides. Latin continued as the international medium of communication in the scholarly world up to the seventeenth century and beyond: for a few purposes it still occupies that position. Great English writers such as Milton were fluent in Latin; in his case the word structure of Latin actually influenced the phrasing of the English poetry. His very title *Paradise Lost* has the same word structure as Latin *paradisus amissus*, which in modern English might be 'the loss of Paradise'.

But the legacy of language goes very much further. In the first place, Latin has given rise to all the Romance languages: French, Italian, Spanish, Portuguese, Rumanian and a few smaller groups. The Romans occupied Dacia, which corresponds roughly to modern Rumania, for only 165 years (AD 105–270); yet they clearly supplanted the language of the Dacians and so imposed Latin that it became the main constituent of the new national language. In so far as English absorbed much of Norman French, it too inherited many words and phrases from Latin. Secondly, learned words from Latin (including some Greek words which Latin incorporated) passed into the vocabulary of European languages; and as new ones came to be needed in botany, medicine and other sciences, they too were mainly based on classical compounds, sometimes (especially recent ones) hybrid, as automobile and television (Greek-Latin), bicycle and radiogram (Latin-Greek). Latin prepositions, roots and word-endings are still being used to form new words. But knowledge of Latin is less widespread than it used to be, and the Latin elements are sometimes combined in untraditional ways. For instance, 'conurbation', from *con-* = *cum*, 'with', *urbs*, 'city', *-atio*, one of the abstract noun endings, would at one time have been formed as 'co-urbation', since *co-*, not *con-*, was always used in compounds where a vowel or *h* followed ('co-operation', 'cohabitation'). Thirdly, in some non-Romance languages in areas not fully occupied by the Romans, things which were imported into the areas by the Romans acquired Latin-based names, eg Welsh *pont* (bridge), *eglwys* (church, Latin from Greek *ecclesia*).

The legacy of Roman law has been extremely long-lasting. It was built into the Code Napoléon, and up to 1900 it operated over a large part of Germany; and although both in France and West Germany new legal codes have been in operation during this century, they incorporate very much of the original Roman corpus. European nations have taken it across the globe; for example, in South Africa, where Roman-Dutch law operates, a knowledge of Latin and of Roman law is indispensable to the legal profession. Nearer home, Scots law, as a result of the Scots' historic links with legal centres in the Low Countries, has more in common with Roman than does English law. The law on which these modern survivals are based is that which prevailed under the emperor Justinian, who in AD 528 ordered a commission in Constantinople to codify all existing laws not older than AD 117, and two years' later a second commission to codify the works of the jurists.

Roman systems of weights, measures and coinage have influenced ours up to decimalisation, and even now the pound sterling remains with its abbreviation £. The Roman *libra*, pound weight (whence our abbreviation lb) came to be used also as a sum of money, from which came *livre* and *lira*; and £ s d stood for *librae, solidi, denarii*. Feet, paces and miles were the standard measurement in Roman times, and the first and last of these have survived, and will for some time as the United States measures have as yet no date for change. On the other hand, the main Roman unit of land measurement, the *iugerum*, was not perpetuated. But it is interesting to note that 'perch', which commonly signified 5½yd (or 5½ × 5½yd), but with local variation, was derived from Latin *pertica*, literally a surveyor's rod.

The legacy of the early Christian Church to Western civilisation is based on three cultures, Jewish, Greek and Roman. Judaea in the time of Christ was a small province of the Roman Empire. Although Christianity first expanded within the Greek world and through the medium of the Greek language, it soon spread to Rome with the missionary activities of St Peter and St Paul. The New Testament was translated into Latin in several versions, of which the Vulgate (Biblia Sacra Vulgata = Holy Bible brought to the people) has been the prevailing one in the West. As Christianity grew in strength, it took over many of the institutions of the Roman Empire. Under Constantine it became the official state religion, and in the period from his reign onwards the pattern of Western Christianity received much of its present mould. St Augustine, who came from North Africa, and many of the other Christian fathers wrote in Latin, though Greek flourished side by side with it. As pagan temples decayed or were pulled down, churches were often built on exactly the same sites, as a symbol of the victory of Christianity incorporating local feelings of the sanctity of shrines. From the division of the Empire into eastern and western halves, and the constant (and sometimes petty) struggles against heresies, emerged a major division of language and rites between the Catholic Church, headed by a Pope in Rome and using mainly Latin as its language, and the Orthodox Church, using at first only Greek. The great expansion of monastic life in the Dark and Middle Ages established some continuity of tradition, as well as attempting to preserve certain aspects of civilisation and tangible remains of Rome. The Church of England, although it broke off from the Roman Church in 1534, preserved more of the institutions and even the wording (though translated) that came down from the Church in early Rome than most other reformed churches of the largely non-Roman language groups.

Study of the classics in the English-speaking world was long linked with the important role given to Greek and Latin in the schools. This reached its culmination in the English public schools of the nineteenth century, in which the most famous educators of the day, such as Arnold of Rugby, saw in Greek and Latin the most important elements in their ideal education. Latin quotations were freely exchanged and understood in Parliament, and administrators were usually expected to have read classics at a university and to have achieved some skill in Greek and Latin composition. The second half of the nineteenth century was the heyday of classical scholarship in Germany and elsewhere. Today, although much classical scholarship is as flourishing as ever, the educational trend is totally different. Only the comparatively few who want to read classics at university are encouraged to, while there is a larger and growing number who are keen to study Greek and Roman civilisation, with none or only the bare minimum of either language, but with the help of many translations. The general public shows a similar trend: books on the ancient world are much read, and translations of the more popular authors are multiplied. When Horace wrote of his odes as *monumentum aere perennius*, 'a monument more durable than bronze', he seemed boastful; but with their 2,000th anniversary in 1978, translation into many languages is bringing them to a wider public than ever before.

### THE LATER EMPIRE

In Chapter 2 the whole period of Rome's expansion from a city to a large empire was outlined. But the Rome which is preserved to us belongs not only to that period but to the centuries which followed that expansion. Today, when we can look back on more recent empires which have contracted, study of the later age of Rome holds for us a certain morbid fascination. From the second half of the second century AD we find Rome increasingly struggling against external enemies.

Marcus Aurelius (emperor AD 161–180), who succeeded Antoninus Pius, was a Stoic philosopher who became embroiled in wars from invading Parthians, Germans and others, in areas where there was no continuous physical barrier against the North and the great heartland of Asia. With barbarians threatening on many sides and armies on such extended and remote fronts, the task of Rome's rulers was not easy. She had the problem of Alexander trying to fix his limits in the East, or much later of Napoleon and Hitler. The material benefits of Roman civilisation led to contentment and some apathy; but there were also movements for separation from Rome, which arose in various provinces from time to time with different measures of success.

With weak or insecure rulers, control of the whole empire was doubly difficult. Marcus Aurelius' son Commodus liked chariot-racing better than governing. In some decades there was a rapid succession of emperors, each meeting a violent death. Meanwhile, partly because of these rapid changes, the bureaucracy became bigger and more complicated all the time. There were continued financial crises (for Diocletian's reaction see Table 2 in Chapter 6), and under Diocletian the Senate was deprived of its right to issue copper coins. Its authority had earlier been weakened when Septimius Severus had replaced senators by *equites* in provincial commands. From 282 even its privilege of conferring the principate on new emperors lapsed. Yet there was always competition to enter the Senate, chiefly because of the personal privileges which membership brought.

Legislation began to affect the customs and actions of citizens in different geographical zones as central control tried to prevent disintegration. A change in the status of free tenants on large estates everywhere occurred in the third century AD. Up to then their personal liberty had been safeguarded. But a new system of tied labour resulted in something approaching serfdom. In the fourth century came another type of infringement of liberty: some tradesmen were compelled to stay in the same type of business and train their sons for it.

Periodic successes in protecting the outer areas are striking. From 208 to 211 Septimius Severus beat back an attack on the North of England by tribes from Scotland and reorganised the defences of Britain, but his invasion of Scotland was unsuccessful. At the end of the third century, attempts by Carausius and Allectus to declare independence in Britain were suppressed by Constantius. At this time and in the fourth century the shores nearest to the Continent (Saxon shore) were fortified against sea raids: ten forts are known, from Brancaster, Norfolk, to Portchester, Hampshire. The recall of legions early in the fifth century was due to Rome's inability to cope with barbarian invasions, and left the island defenceless against raids across the North Sea.

Septimius Severus was active on other fronts too. He and his son Caracalla constructed a long *limes*, boundary line with earth ramparts, in the Danube basin and another in North Africa. Aurelian not only fortified Rome but defeated the queen regent of Palmyra, Zenobia, whose life he chivalrously spared.

Diocletian showed great administrative ability, and in an attempt at more effective control and government divided the Empire into two more manageable parts, himself taking the eastern half and Maximian the western, and appointing 'Caesars', ie subordinate emperors, under the eastern and the western Augustus. The great achievements of Constantine (emperor 306–337) were the founding of Constantinople, called the new Rome, at Byzantium and the encouragement of Christianity, which in his reign became the official religion of the Roman Empire. During all this period a careerist from any province stood a good chance of becoming emperor: Septimius Severus was born at Lepcis Magna, North Africa, Aurelian in Dacia, Diocletian in Dalmatia, Constantine at Naissus (Niš).

Why did the western Empire decline and fall to barbarians in the fifth century? Some have tried to give medical reasons, such as malaria or lead-poisoning. Others hold that by persistent harassing the barbarians, to whom the wealth and more advanced economies must have been a lure, eventually made Roman positions untenable, or that Rome's concepts of citizenship and rights played into the hands of barbarians by permitting the appointment of generals of barbarian origin, who were secretly working against Rome. The western regions were more accessible, it seems, to less fortunate and less civilised peoples; while strong coastal fortresses like Diocletian's palace at Split were able to defy them. Ancient historians were inclined to blame moral lapses. Gibbon blamed Christianity, but in that case, as A. H. M. Jones put it: 'Why did not the more Christian east, with its much more virulent theological disputes, fall first?' With twentieth-century parallels in mind, we may perhaps agree with modern historians who put the greatest blame on general apathy and the reluctance of men in threatened areas to pull together. Even if ambitious provincials were energetic, the ordinary man in Gaul, Spain or North Africa was not likely to dash to arms to repel a barbarian invasion. In 376, when the Goths invaded Thrace, the army was inefficient because many officers were chiefly interested in the money to be made out of slave-dealing. It was not the sack of

Rome in the early fifth century that spelt the end of the western Empire, but a whole series of disasters which followed. Gibbon may be allowed the last word: 'Instead of enquiring why the Roman empire was destroyed, we should rather be surprised that it had subsisted so long.'

# Chronological Table

ONLY the more important dates are recorded. In the late Empire the names and dates of only a few emperors are given.

| BC | |
|---|---|
| 753 | Traditional date of foundation of Rome |
| 510–509 | Traditional date of expulsion of kings and start of republic |
| 431 | Defeat of Aequi |
| 396 | Capture of Veii |
| 390 or | |
| 387 | Sack of Rome by the Gauls |
| 367 | Plebeians gain rights |
| 343–290 | Intermittent wars: First Samnite War, Latin War, Second and Third Samnite Wars |
| 338 | Foundation of colony at Antium (Ostia founded about the same time) |
| 329 | Foundation of colony at Anxur-Tarracina |
| 312 | Northern stretch of Via Appia built |
| 282–275 | War against King Pyrrhus of Epirus |
| 264–241 | First Punic War |
| 263 | First public sundial in Rome |
| c242–c204 | Livius Andronicus in Rome |
| 218–201 | Second Punic War |
| 197 | Defeat of King Philip V of Macedon |
| 196–191 | Conquest of Cisalpine Gaul |
| 186 | Senate decree on worship of Bacchus |
| 186 | Defeat of King Perseus of Macedon |

| 159 | First public water-clock in Rome |
| 156–155 | Visit of Carneades to Rome |
| 149–146 | Third Punic War |
| 146 | Destruction of Carthage and Corinth |
| 133 | Successful siege of Numantia, Spain. King Attalus III of Pergamum leaves his kingdom to Rome. Tiberius Gracchus tribune of the people |
| 123–122 | Gaius Gracchus tribune of the people. Colony founded at Carthage |
| 112–105 | War against Jugurtha of Numidia |
| 102–101 | Marius defeats Teutones and Cimbri |
| 91–87 | Social War (ie against *socii*, allies) |
| 88–85, | |
| 81, | |
| 74–63 | Wars against Mithridates in Asia Minor |
| 82–80 | Sulla in power |
| 73–70 | Spartacus' slave revolt |
| 67 | Pirates crushed |
| 63 | Cicero's consulship. Catilinarian conspiracy |
| 60 | First triumvirate formed: Pompey, Caesar, Crassus |
| 58–49 | Caesar's Gallic Wars (raids on Britain 55–54) |
| 53 | Crassus defeated at Carrhae, Parthia, and killed |
| 49–36, | |
| 32–31 | Civil wars |
| 48–44 | Caesar in power |
| 44 | Assassination of Caesar |
| 43 | Second triumvirate formed: Antony, Octavian, Lepidus. Death of Cicero, proscribed by triumvirs |
| 42 | Defeat of Brutus and Cassius at Philippi, Macedonia |
| 31 | Battle of Actium (defeat of Antony by Octavian) |
| 30 | Death of Antony and Cleopatra. Annexation of Egypt |
| 27– | |
| AD 14 | Augustus (formerly Octavian) emperor |
| 23 | Permanent settlement of the emperor's position |
| 20–19 | Agreement with Parthia |
| 19 | Death of Virgil |
| 4 | Probable date of Christ's birth |

AD

| | |
|---|---|
| 9 | Ambush of three legions under Varus in Germany |
| 14–37 | Tiberius emperor |
| 26 | Tiberius retires to Capri |
| 31 | Fall of Sejanus |
| 37–41 | Gaius (Caligula) emperor |
| 41–54 | Claudius emperor |
| 43 | Invasion of Britain |
| 54–68 | Nero emperor |
| 60 | Boudicca's revolt in Britain |
| 64 | Great fire of Rome |
| 65 | Pisonian conspiracy |
| 68–69 | Galba emperor |
| 69 | Otho and Vitellius emperors. Revolt in Gaul |
| 69–79 | Vespasian emperor |
| 70 | Siege of Jerusalem |
| 78–84 | Agricola governor of Britain |
| 79–81 | Titus emperor |
| 79 | Eruption of Vesuvius |
| 81–96 | Domitian emperor |
| 96–98 | Nerva emperor |
| 98–117 | Trajan emperor |
| 101–105 | Dacian Wars |
| 117–138 | Hadrian emperor |
| 122–126 | Hadrian's Wall built |
| 138–161 | Antoninus Pius emperor |
| 161–180 | Marcus Aurelius sole or joint emperor |
| 177–192 | Commodus joint or sole emperor |
| 193–211 | Septimius Severus sole or joint emperor |
| 198–217 | Caracalla joint or sole emperor |
| 212 | General grant of Roman citizenship |
| 218–222 | Elagabalus emperor |
| 270–275 | Aurelian emperor |
| 271–275 | Rome fortified |
| 284–305 | Diocletian sole or joint emperor |
| 301 | Diocletian's edict on maximum prices |
| 306–337 | Constantine I joint or sole emperor |

312      Battle of the Mulvian Bridge

325      First council of Nicaea: Christianity becomes the official religion of the Empire

324–330  Foundation of Constantinople (original name Byzantium)

361–363  Julian emperor

379–395  Theodosius I joint emperor

383–408  Arcadius joint emperor and emperor of the East

393–423  Honorius joint emperor and emperor of the West

410      Sack of Rome by the Goths. Approximate end of military occupation of Britain

475–476  Romulus Augustulus last emperor of the West (not recognised in the East)

527–565  Justinian emperor

533      Codification of Roman law

535–540  Italy reconquered from the Ostrogoths by forces of the emperor Justinian in Constantinople

# Bibliography

ADCOCK, SIR F. E. *The Roman Art of War under the Republic* (Cambridge, 1960)

BALSDON, J. P. V. D. *Roman Women: Their History and Habits* (London, 1962)

——. *Life and Leisure in Ancient Rome* (London, 1969)

——. *Roman Civilisation* (Harmondsworth, Middx, 1969)

BEARE, W. *The Roman Stage* (London, 3rd ed, 1965)

BIRLEY, A. R. *Life in Roman Britain* (London and New York, 1964)

BOAK, A. E. R. and SINNIGEN, W. G. *A History of Rome to AD 565* (New York and London, 5th ed, 1965)

BRUNT, P. A. *Italian Manpower, 225 BC–AD 14* (Oxford, 1971)

BURFORD, ALISON. *Craftsmen in Greek and Roman Society* (London, 1972)

CARCOPINO, J. *Daily Life in Ancient Rome*, ed H. T. Rowell, trans E. O. Lorimer (Harmondsworth, Middx, 1967)

CHEVALLIER, R. *Les voies romaines* (Paris, 1972)

COWELL, F. R. *Everyday Life in Ancient Rome* (London and New York, 6th imp, 1970)

CROOK, J. A. *Law and Life of Rome* (London, 1967)

DILKE, O. A. W. *The Roman Land Surveyors* (Newton Abbot, 1971)

DUDLEY, D. R. *Urbs Roma* (Aberdeen, 1967)

DUFF, J. WIGHT. *Literary History of Rome from the Origins to the Close of the Golden Age* (London, 1909; rev A. M. Duff, 1960)

——. *Literary History of Rome in the Silver Age* (London, 1927; rev A. M. Duff, 1964)

DUNCAN-JONES, R. *The Economy of the Roman Empire* (Cambridge, 1974)

EARL, D. C. *The Moral and Political Tradition of Rome* (London, 1967)

——. *The Age of Augustus* (London, 1968)

FERGUSON, J. *The Religions of the Roman Empire* (London, 1970)

FINLEY, M. I. *Slavery in Classical Antiquity* (Cambridge, 1960; rev 1968)

GRANT, M. *Gladiators* (London, 1967)

——. *Roman History from Coins* (Cambridge, 1968)

GRIMAL, P. *The Civilisation of Rome*, trans W. S. Maguinness (London, 1963)

HEYDEN, A. A. H. VAN DER and SCULLARD, H. H. *An Atlas of the Classical World* (London, 1959)

HIGHET, G. *The Classical Tradition* (Oxford, 1949)

JENNISON, G. *Animals for Show and Pleasure in Ancient Rome* (Manchester, 1937)

LIVERSIDGE, JOAN. *Britain in the Roman Empire* (London, 1968)

MARROU, H. I. *A History of Education in Antiquity*, trans G. Lamb (New York, 1964)

MORITZ, L. A. *Grain-mills and Flour in Classical Antiquity* (Oxford, 1958)

OGILVIE, R. M. *The Romans and Their Gods in the Age of Augustus* (London, 1969)

——. *Latin and Greek: A History of the Influence of the Classics on English Life from 1600 to 1918* (London, 1964)

*Oxford Classical Dictionary*, ed N. G. L. Hammond and H. H. Scullard (Oxford, 2nd ed, 1970)

SALMON, E. T. *Roman Colonisation under the Republic* (London, 1969)

SANDYS, SIR J. E. *A Companion to Latin Studies* (Cambridge, 3rd ed, 1929)

SCARBOROUGH, J. *Roman Medicine* (London, 1969)

SCULLARD, H. H. *From the Gracchi to Nero* (London, 2nd ed, 1963)

STARR, C. G. *The Ancient Romans* (New York and London, 1971)

TANZER, HELEN H. *The Common People of Pompeii* (Baltimore, 1939)

THOMSON, J. O. *Everyman's Classical Atlas* (London, 1961)

TOYNBEE, JOCELYN M. C. *Roman Art* (London, 1965)

——. *Death and Burial in the Roman World* (London, 1971)

WATSON, G. R. *The Roman Soldier* (London, 1961)

WHEELER, SIR R. E. Mortimer. *Rome beyond the Imperial Frontiers* (London, 1954)

WHITE, K. D. *Roman Farming* (London, 1970)

The best bibliography of current classical studies is *L'Année Philologique*, published annually in Paris

# Index

F